TRANSPORTATION INFRASTRU                    ES,
AIRPORTS

# TRANSIT SYSTEM RESILIENCE

## DEVELOPMENT EFFORTS
## AND CHALLENGES

TRANSPORTATION INFRASTRUCTURE - ROADS, HIGHWAYS, BRIDGES,
AIRPORTS AND MASS TRANSIT

# TRANSIT SYSTEM RESILIENCE

# DEVELOPMENT EFFORTS
# AND CHALLENGES

## KAYLA HODGES
### EDITOR

*New York*

# CONTENTS

# PREFACE

This book examines how DHS and DOT help transit agencies make their systems resilient; actions selected transit agencies take to make their systems resilient; and challenges transit agencies face with making their systems resilient. It also addresses the progress the Department of Transportation has made allocating, obligating, and disbursing the Disaster Relief Appropriations Act surface transportation funds; how the Federal Transit Administration's (FTA) new Public Transportation Emergency Relief program compares to the Federal Emergency Management Agency's (FEMA) and Federal Highway Administration's (FHWA)emergency relief programs; and the extent to which FTA and FEMA have implemented their memorandum of agreement to coordinate their roles and responsibilities when providing assistance to transit agencies.

Chapter 1 – Public transit systems, which receive funding from the federal government, are vulnerable to catastrophic events, as demonstrated by the impact Hurricane Sandy and other events have had on transit systems. These events highlight our reliance on transit systems for access to jobs, medical care, and other services, as well as the cost of recovering from these events. For instance, of the $50.5 billion Congress appropriated to help communities devastated by Sandy, $10.9 billion was provided for disaster relief to public transit agencies. Building resilience—the ability to prepare for, respond to, recover from, and mitigate the risk of catastrophic events—is one strategy to help limit the nation's fiscal exposure to catastrophic events.

GAO was asked to review transit system resilience to catastrophic events. This report examines (1) how DHS and DOT help transit agencies make their systems resilient; (2) actions selected transit agencies take to make their systems resilient; and (3) challenges transit agencies face with making their systems resilient. GAO examined documentation and interviewed officials from DHS and DOT, and officials from nine transit and five emergency management agencies.GAO selected a non-generalizable sample of agencies in five locations, chosen for transit ridership volume and variation in geography, types of risks, and transit modes.

GAO did not make any recommendations in this report. DHS and DOT provided technical comments, which were incorporated as appropriate.

Chapter 2 – In October 2012, Hurricane Sandy devastated portions of the Mid-Atlantic coast causing severe damage to transit facilities and infrastructure and disrupting mobility in the New York metropolitan region. In January 2013, the President signed the DRAA, which provided approximately $50.5 billion in federal aid for expenses related to Hurricane Sandy. GAO was asked to examine DRAA emergency relief assistance for transportation.

This report addresses (1) the progress DOT has made allocating, obligating, and disbursing DRAA surface transportation funds, (2) how FTA's new Public Transportation Emergency Relief program compares to FEMA's and FHWA's emergency relief programs, and (3) the extent to which FTA and FEMA have implemented their memorandum of agreement to coordinate their roles and responsibilities when providing assistance to transit agencies. GAO analyzed relevant laws, regulations, and agency documentation, and interviewed DOT, FEMA, and New Jersey and New York area transit officials.

In: Transit System Resilience
Editor: Kayla Hodges

ISBN: 978-1-63482-567-2
© 2015 Nova Science Publishers, Inc.

*Chapter 1*

# PUBLIC TRANSIT: FEDERAL AND TRANSIT AGENCIES TAKING STEPS TO BUILD TRANSIT SYSTEMS' RESILIENCE BUT FACE CHALLENGES[*]

## *United States Government Accountability Office*

### ABBREVIATIONS

| | |
|------|------|
| BASE | Baseline Assessment for Security Enhancement |
| CDBG | Community Development Block Grant |
| DHS | Department of Homeland Security |
| DOT | Department of Transportation |
| DRAA | Disaster Relief Appropriations Act |
| ERP | Emergency Relief Program |
| FEMA | Federal Emergency Management Agency |
| FHWA | Federal Highway Administration |
| FMA | Flood Mitigation Assistance |
| FTA | Federal Transit Administration |
| HMGP | Hazard Mitigation Grant Program |
| MAP-21 | Moving Ahead for Progress in the 21st Century Act |

---

[*] This is an edited, reformatted and augmented version of a report, GAO-15-159, issued by the Government Accountability Office, dated December 2014.

| MOU | memorandum of understanding |
|---|---|
| PDM | Pre-Disaster Mitigation |
| SEPTA | Southeastern Pennsylvania Transportation Authority |
| TRB | Transportation Research Board |
| TSA | Transportation Security Administration |
| TSGP | Transit Security Grant Program |
| TTAL | Top Transit Asset List |
| WMATA | Washington Metropolitan Area Transit Authority |

# WHY GAO DID THIS STUDY

Public transit systems, which receive funding from the federal government, are vulnerable to catastrophic events, as demonstrated by the impact Hurricane Sandy and other events have had on transit systems. These events highlight our reliance on transit systems for access to jobs, medical care, and other services, as well as the cost of recovering from these events. For instance, of the $50.5 billion Congress appropriated to help communities devastated by Sandy, $10.9 billion was provided for disaster relief to public transit agencies. Building resilience—the ability to prepare for, respond to, recover from, and mitigate the risk of catastrophic events—is one strategy to help limit the nation's fiscal exposure to catastrophic events.

GAO was asked to review transit system resilience to catastrophic events. This report examines (1) how DHS and DOT help transit agencies make their systems resilient; (2) actions selected transit agencies take to make their systems resilient; and (3) challenges transit agencies face with making their systems resilient. GAO examined documentation and interviewed officials from DHS and DOT, and officials from nine transit and five emergency management agencies.GAO selected a non-generalizable sample of agencies in five locations, chosen for transit ridership volume and variation in geography, types of risks, and transit modes.

GAO did not make any recommendations in this report. DHS and DOT provided technical comments, which were incorporated as appropriate.

# WHAT GAO FOUND

The Departments of Homeland Security (DHS) and Transportation (DOT) provide funding and other support to transit agencies to help make their systems resilient to catastrophic events. DHS focuses on emergency management and security, and provides funding through its hazard-mitigation, transit-security, and other grant programs. DOT's Federal Transit Administration (FTA) provides support through formula and discretionary-funding programs for transit capital-investment projects and for improving and maintaining existing systems. Both DHS and DOT provide transit agencies with technical assistance, such as for security programs or climate-change adaptation efforts.

Transit agencies that GAO selected identified a number of actions they are taking to help make their systems more resilient, including performing risk assessments and developing plans, such as emergency operations plans. These agencies also take actions, such as building redundant assets or facilities, to ensure the continuity of operations of the agencies' systems. Further, transit agencies have changed their infrastructure to mitigate the potential impact of disasters on their assets. For example, one agency elevated vents and curbs to minimize water flowing into the subway.

Although all transit agencies GAO selected are taking resilience-building actions, officials GAO interviewed said that transit agencies face challenges with placing priorities on resilience and with certain aspects of some grant programs. In particular, officials from DHS, DOT, and transit agencies GAO selected explained that it is difficult for transit agencies to place priority on resilience activities because managers may be reluctant to focus on resilience and resilience activities compete with other priorities for funding. Federal, transit-agency, and emergency-management officials also cited challenges related to some aspects of federal grants that have made it difficult for transit agencies to, among other things, incorporate resilience into disaster recovery efforts and make regional transit-networks resilient. DHS, DOT, and some transit agencies are taking some actions to address these challenges, such as developing tools to help management prioritize resilience activities.

* * *

December 10, 2014

The Honorable Tim Johnson
Chairman
Committee on Banking, Housing, and Urban Affairs
United States Senate

The Honorable Robert Menendez
Chairman
Subcommittee on Housing, Transportation and Community Development
Committee on Banking, Housing, and Urban Affairs
United States Senate

In recent years, the federal government, in addition to the over $10 billion that the Department of Transportation (DOT) provides annually to transit agencies for their systems, has provided billions of dollars to help transit agencies recover from catastrophic events,[1] such as Hurricane Sandy.[2] For example, $10.9 billion of the $50.5 billion Congress appropriated to help communities devastated by Hurricane Sandy was provided to help affected public transit agencies repair and make their transit facilities resilient to future disasters.[3,4] In addition to the financial impact, loss of transit services, and damage of related infrastructure can have negative effects on a community by impeding access to jobs, medical care, education, shopping, and other services. For example, recent severe weather events, such as major winter storms in Massachusetts and landslides in Washington State, temporarily shut down transit systems in these areas. Further, these types of weather-related events can be expected to increase. According to the United States Global Change Research Program,[5] the impacts and costs of weather disasters are likely to increase in significance as such events become more common and intense due to climate change.[6] Transit systems' vulnerability results, in part, from their open nature, the large geographic areas they cover, and the critical transportation service they provide millions of people.

The Department of Homeland Security (DHS), DOT, and the over 2,000 public transit agencies across the country play a role in minimizing transit systems' vulnerabilities to catastrophic events and helping ensure that transit agencies are resilient to all types of hazards caused by nature and people. Resilience is the capability to prepare for, respond to, recover from, and mitigate the risk of catastrophic events.[7] We previously have recommended building resilience—such as taking actions to mitigate vulnerabilities to severe weather events—as one strategy to help limit the nation's fiscal exposure as a result of catastrophic events.[8] In addition, we identified challenges to building resilience, including (1) communities balancing the need to invest in hazard mitigation with other economic development goals and (2) the clarity of information needed to inform risk-based decision making.[9] Such challenges may affect the extent to which public transit agencies are resilient to catastrophic events.

Given the importance of public transit agencies and their vulnerability to adverse weather and other catastrophic events that disrupt transit services and damage transit infrastructure and investments, you asked us to identify how public transit agencies make their systems resilient to catastrophic events. This report examines (1) how DHS and DOT help transit agencies make their systems resilient to catastrophic events; (2) actions selected transit agencies take to make their systems resilient; and (3) challenges transit agencies face with making their systems resilient to such events. Our review focuses on all-hazard catastrophic events; that is, those caused either by nature (e.g., hurricanes, flooding, fires) or by humans (e.g., security events, including terrorism).

To determine the activities DHS and DOT take to help transit agencies make their systems more resilient to catastrophic events, we reviewed and analyzed documentation from the two federal agencies on their relevant programs, requirements, guidance, policies, and technical assistance. We also interviewed officials from these two agencies.[10] To identify actions selected transit agencies take to make their systems more resilient, we reviewed documentation and interviewed officials from nine transit agencies and five local emergency management offices in five metropolitan areas: Los Angeles Region, California; Miami, Florida; Philadelphia, Pennsylvania; Seattle/Puget Sound Region, Washington; and Washington, D.C. These areas are among the 10 largest metropolitan areas in terms of transit ridership and were selected to obtain variation in geography, types of risks, and transit modes.[11] In each metropolitan area, we selected transit agencies that had relatively high ridership and were located in the selected city itself or provided service to the city. The nine transit agencies, which we visited, are listed below.

- Los Angeles County Metropolitan Transportation Authority (Los Angeles Region, California);

- Orange County Transportation Authority (Los Angeles Region, California);
- Southern California Regional Rail Authority (Metrolink) (Los Angeles Region, California);
- Miami-Dade Transit (Miami, Florida);
- Southeastern Pennsylvania Transportation Authority (SEPTA) (Philadelphia, Pennsylvania);
- Washington State Ferries (Seattle/Puget Sound Region, Washington);
- King County Metro Transit (Seattle/Puget Sound Region, Washington);
- Sound Transit (Seattle/Puget Sound Region, Washington); and
- Washington Metropolitan Area Transit Authority (WMATA) (Washington, D.C.).

While the information we obtained from the five metropolitan areas is not generalizable to transit systems nationwide, the selected areas have some of the larger transit systems in terms of ridership. To identify challenges transit agencies face with making their systems resilient to catastrophic events, we interviewed officials from DOT, DHS, the nine transit agencies, five emergency management offices, and four researchers knowledgeable in transit systems, emergency management, or federal transportation programs. We analyzed the information gained from these interviews to identify the most frequently cited challenges. Appendix I describes our objectives, scope, and methodology in greater detail.

We conducted this performance audit from October 2013 through December 2014 in accordance with generally accepted government auditing standards. Those standards require that we plan and perform the audit to obtain sufficient, appropriate evidence to provide a reasonable basis for our findings and conclusions based on our audit objectives. We believe that the evidence obtained provides a reasonable basis for our findings and conclusions on our audit objectives.

## BACKGROUND

In response to the risks posed by man-made and natural disasters, such as acts of terrorism and severe weather, over the past decade the federal government has emphasized the need to improve the resilience of the nation's critical infrastructure through various national policies (see table 1). These policies—which focus on critical infrastructure, national preparedness, and climate change or weather-related events—address resilience in the context of homeland security (e.g., terrorism) and natural disasters. The federal government has targeted 16 critical infrastructure areas for resilience-building policies. Transportation infrastructure, which includes public transit systems, is one of these areas.[12]

**Table 1. National Policies That Emphasize Resilience of the Nation's Critical Infrastructure, Including Public Transit**

| Focus of national policy | National policy | Purpose |
|---|---|---|
| Critical Infrastructure | Homeland Security Presidential Directive-7: Critical Infrastructure Identification, Prioritization, and Protection Issued on December 17, 2003 | Designates the nation's mass transit systems, among other types of transportation systems, as critical infrastructure. |
| | National Infrastructure Protection Plan 2013: Partnering for Critical Infrastructure Security and Resiliencen Issued in 2006 and updated in 2009 and 2013 | A strategic framework that describes how federal, state, and local government and private sector, and non-profit participants should work together to manage risks and achieve security and resilience outcomes in critical infrastructure. |
| | Presidential Policy Directive-21: Critical Infrastructure Security and Resilience Issued on February 12, 2013 | Establishes a national policy on critical infrastructure security and resilience. |
| National preparedness | National Security Presidential Directive51/Homeland Security Presidential Directive20: National Continuity Policy Issued May 9, 2007 | Establishes a comprehensive national policy to help ensure the continuity of essential functions following an emergency. |
| | Presidential Policy Directive-8: National Preparedness Issued on March 30, 2011 | Identifies the need for a national preparedness goal and strategy aimed at strengthening the nation's security and resilience through systematicpreparations against terrorist acts and catastrophic |

**Table 1. (Continued)**

| Focus of national policy | National policy | Purpose |
|---|---|---|
| | | natural disasters, among other things. This policy directive replaced Homeland Security Presidential Directive-8: National Preparedness, which was issued on December 17, 2003. |
| Climate change or weatherrelated events | Department of Transportation Policy Statement on Climate Change Adaptation Issued in June 2011 | States that DOT shall consider climate change impacts on current systems and future investments, and incorporate climate adaptation strategies into its transportation missions, programs, and operations. This policy statement is in the process of being updated. |
| | Executive Order 13632: Establishing the Hurricane Sandy Rebuilding Task Force Issued on December 7, 2012 | Establishes the Hurricane Sandy Rebuilding Task Force to provide coordination necessary to support long-term rebuilding in the affected areas. |
| | Executive Order 13653: Preparing the United States for the Impacts of Climate Change Issued on November 6, 2013 | Directs the federal government to pursue new strategies to improve the nation's preparedness and resilience to the impacts of climate change, including in the area of critical infrastructure. |

Source: GAO analysis. | GAO-15-159.

Actions that can help transit agencies prepare for, respond to, recover from, and mitigate the risk of catastrophic events can contribute to transit system resilience.[13] These actions can be taken before, during, and after an event (see fig. 1). For example, transit agencies can develop plans to help them prepare for a catastrophic event before it occurs, and can repair transit infrastructure after an event so that the infrastructure can better withstand similar events in the future.

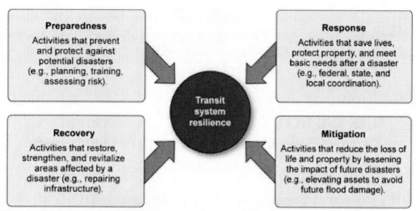

Source: GAO analysis of DHS socumentation on addressing risks.| GAO-15-159.

Figure 1. Actions That Can Contribute to Transit System Resilience.

In large part, the actions for resilience-building efforts noted in figure 1 occur at the local level and are specific to the needs, scope, and risks of the transit systems, factoring in state and local priorities. However, the Stafford Act of 1988, as amended,[14] mandated a role for the federal government in assisting state and local governments to carry out their responsibilities to alleviate the damage from disasters. Today, federal agencies—DHS and DOT, in particular—share federal oversight of and assistance for critical infrastructure, including transit systems.[15] Moreover, DHS and DOT are the federal agencies responsible under the National Infrastructure Protection Plan for promoting national resilience-related polices in public transit systems. DHS has primary responsibility for transportation security and emergency preparedness and response. DHS's Transportation Security Administration (TSA) is the primary federal agency overseeing security matters for public transit systems and provides technical assistance to transit agencies to augment their system security.[16] DHS's Federal Emergency Management Agency (FEMA) has responsibility for administering the public transportation-security grant provisions of the 9-11 Act[17] and is the lead federal agency responsible for building the nation's capability to prepare for and respond to all-hazards catastrophic events. Transit agencies can apply to FEMA for grants for emergency planning, response, recovery, and mitigation efforts—either directly or through their states, depending on the type of grant. DOT's Federal Transit Administration (FTA) provides funds to help develop new transit systems and improve, maintain, and operate existing systems; and provides technical assistance as needed to transit systems. As specified by law,[18] FTA's programs for funding transit systems operate as either formula or discretionary grants[19] for certain types of capital or operating expenses.[20] As discussed below, until recently FTA did not have funds authorized specifically for resilience or disaster assistance for transit systems.

# DHS AND DOT ASSISTANCE CAN CONTRIBUTE TO TRANSIT SYSTEM RESILIENCE; HOWEVER, SOME LIMITATIONS EXIST

## DHS Assistance Focuses on Security and Emergency Management

Created to strengthen the security of the nation's transportation systems, TSA sets priorities for protecting and evaluating the security of public transit systems. FEMA, as the federal agency responsible for emergency management, has certain grant programs that provide funds that may be used for transit systems' resilience-related activities both before and after catastrophic events. As noted by DHS and transit officials, some changes in funding levels and timing of grant availability can limit transit agency and local use of federal assistance.

### TSA

According to DHS officials, TSA employs a risk-based strategy to determine security risks on public transit systems. DHS maintains a Top Transit Asset List (TTAL) to identify critical infrastructure assets that are vital to the continuity of major transit systems and whose destruction would be detrimental to the region and even the nation. TSA uses the TTAL to help target technical assistance, and FEMA uses it to allocate transit security grants to reduce risks associated with major transit systems, especially in large metropolitan areas.

As part of its risk-based approach, TSA conducts 30 to 34 Baseline Assessment for Security Enhancement (BASE) reviews of public transit agencies per year, which support transit agency resilience in several ways.[21] For example, TSA uses BASE to evaluate the efficiency and effectiveness of transit agencies' security and emergency response programs and to identify existing security guidelines and requirements and security gaps so the evaluated transit agency can prioritize actions to address vulnerabilities to enhance security. Officials from DHS and transit agencies we visited said that the BASE reviews are an effective tool to assess a transit agency's security program. According to DHS officials, DHS also uses the results of the BASE reviews in the selection process for Transit Security Grant Program (TSGP) grants; the TSGP is discussed further below. Furthermore, TSA disseminates best practices, identified in part through the BASE program, among regional and national transit agencies, emergency management agencies, and state agencies, which can help make transit systems more resilient. These best practices include, for example, incorporating resilience into capital project design. Moreover, DHS has stated that, as critical infrastructure is built and refurbished, those involved in making design decisions should consider the most effective ways to prepare for threats and hazards, mitigate vulnerabilities, and minimize consequences.

### *FEMA*

FEMA administers several grant programs that transit agencies can to apply for to improve the resilience of their systems. The Transit Security Grant Program (TSGP) 22 is a competitive program for funding projects to reduce risks associated with potential terrorist attacks and to increase the resilience of transit and other forms of critical infrastructure. Projects include installing security cameras and providing security training for transit employees. For instance, King County Metro in the Seattle/Puget Sound Region received a TSGP grant for cameras, dogs for bomb detection, and overtime costs for security staff. In addition, transit agencies that receive TSGP grants are required to take actions before applying to receive the grants to plan for and help mitigate the impact of events on transit systems. These actions include developing security plans and conducting risk assessments to identify vulnerabilities and weaknesses in security, such as in emergency response planning and employee training. Transit agencies that receive TSGP grants are required by FEMA policy to use their grants within 2 years of receiving them, although transit agencies may request an extension through a formal request to FEMA that describes why an extension is needed.[23]

TSGP funds for public transit peaked in fiscal year 2009 at almost $500 million, but were at or below $90 million in each of the past 3 fiscal years. [24] See figure 2 for the annual TSGP amounts awarded for public transit from fiscal year 2005 through fiscal year 2014—the current year. Later in this report, we discuss the challenges experienced by transit agencies related to the timing of these grant funds. To determine which transit agencies receive TSGP funds, a panel of officials from different DHS agencies, including FEMA and

TSA, rank and score proposed projects based on, among other things, whether agencies have assets listed in the TTAL and their BASE results.[25]

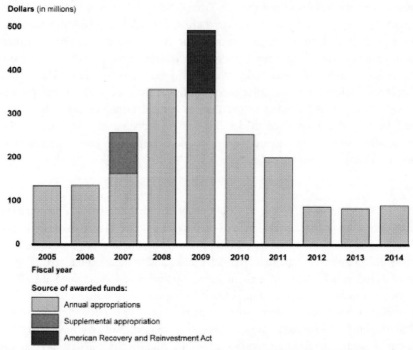

Source: GAO analysis of funding data provided by DHS on the TSGP.| GAO-15-159.

Figure 2. Transit Security Grant Program (TSGP) Funds Awarded for Public Transit, Fiscal Years 2005 through 2014.

FEMA also administers a Port Security Grant Program, designed to directly support maritime transportation-infrastructure security activities, such as improvement of port-wide maritime security-risk management, maritime security-training exercises, and maritime security-mitigation protocols that support port recovery and resilience capabilities. According to DHS officials, ferry systems that are awarded these funds cannot also apply for TSGP funds for the same project.

In addition to the TSGP and Port Security Grant Program, transit agencies are eligible for the Homeland Security Grant Program. These grants, such as the Urban Areas Security Initiative, are aimed at helping metropolitan areas build and sustain national preparedness. However, transit agencies cannot apply directly for these funds. State Administrative Agencies apply for these grants on behalf of the state and its subgrantees, including transit agencies and other local entities seeking such funds.

FEMA's disaster- and hazard-mitigation grant programs can also be used for helping make transit systems resilient. Public Assistance, typically the largest of these programs, focuses on immediate post-disaster recovery efforts and its grants can be used for removing debris, implementing emergency protective measures, and repairing or replacing damaged public equipment or facilities. Public Assistance funds also may be used for hazard mitigation measures to damaged infrastructure to reduce the likelihood of future damage. According to FEMA officials, transit agencies are also eligible for three FEMA mitigation grant programs—Hazard Mitigation Grant Program (HMGP), Pre-Disaster Mitigation (PDM) Program, and Flood Mitigation Assistance (FMA) Program—that primarily fund weather-related resilience efforts, such as implementing flood control measures or protection from the effects of earthquakes. Transit agencies in the wake of recent disasters have used mitigation funds to support resilience projects.[26]

While FEMA's mitigation grant programs can help transit agencies carry out resilience-type projects, we identified two limitations transit agencies face in trying to obtain such funds. First, to obtain FEMA funding, transit agencies must apply through their state government as opposed to applying directly to the federal government. Thus, transit agencies are competing with other state and local organizations, including non-transitrelated organizations such as housing organizations and public utilities, for FEMA funds. Second, FEMA officials noted that because various FEMA grants and other federal funds to aid recovery and resilience building after a catastrophic event have different regulations and timeframes, it could be difficult for the grant recipients to coordinate the use of these funds for resilience efforts.[27] We will discuss challenges that transit agencies and others indicate arise from competing priorities and the timing of federal grants in more detail later in the report.

## DOT Focuses on Transit Funding and Technical Assistance

### *FTA Formula and Discretionary Funds*

DOT provides funding and technical assistance to transit agencies to improve their resilience. DOT requires that transit agencies with light rail, heavy rail, or other rail "fixed-guideway systems" have hazard and emergency management programs, and develop security plans.[28] As we discussed above, actions that help transit agencies prepare for catastrophic events, such as developing plans, can help build transit system resilience.

FTA provides financial assistance through various formula and discretionary programs for transit capital-investment projects and for improving and maintaining existing systems. All of these programs, except for the new Public Transportation Emergency Relief Program (ERP), allow but do not provide specifically for improvements for transit systems' resilience to catastrophic events. However, according to FTA officials, activities to build resilience in transit systems are eligible capital expenses under these programs. For example, a transit agency could use Section 5339—Bus and Bus Facilities Program funds[29] to build a new bus facility on higher land to make it less vulnerable to floods.

FTA grantees are responsible for managing their programs in accordance with federal requirements, and FTA is responsible for ensuring that grantees follow federal statutory and administrative requirements. While FTA does not require transit agencies' use of such grants for resilience projects, FTA officials said that one way to ensure that transit agencies practice resilience is the grant requirement [30] that grantees maintain FTAfunded assets in good operating order for the duration of their "useful life" or expected period of service. FTA may require that transit agencies refund FTA for the portion of an FTA-paid asset if that asset does not last the minimal life cycle for that asset. FTA officials stated that this requirement could incentivize transit agencies to take actions that could contribute to system resilience. For example, the useful life requirement could encourage transit agencies to adopt improved asset management practices, which also improve the resilience of transit assets.[31] However, in cases of disasters, FTA can waive this requirement. FTA waived this requirement for the buses that were destroyed by Hurricane Katrina and thus were taken out of service before reaching their minimum useful life. FTA officials further told us that, as permitted under the Stafford Act, FTA waived the remaining useful life for property damaged or destroyed by Hurricane Sandy.

In addition to federal requirements, FTA officials told us that local building codes and current industry design standards could help transit agencies build resilience. For instance, according to transit officials we spoke with in California, California's stringent seismic codes enable transit systems to build to better withstand earthquakes. Research has shown that design improvements have resulted in stronger, more resilient transit vehicles that can better withstand terrorist attacks.

### FTA Emergency and Disaster-Related Fund

Among other things, the Moving Ahead for Progress in the 21st Century Act (MAP-21) authorized the Public Transportation Emergency Relief Program (ERP) within FTA, which provides grants for, among other things, capital projects to protect, repair, reconstruct, or replace equipment and facilities of public transportation systems that the DOT Secretary determines are in danger of suffering serious damage, or have suffered serious damage, as a result of an emergency.[32] A transit agency can apply directly for these grants without having to go through its state government (as required for most FEMA grants). Under the FTA ERP, damaged or threatened transit equipment and facilities can be repaired as well as made more resilient to current and future conditions and risks. Further, operating costs to cover evacuation activities, rescue operations, and temporary transit services are also eligible uses of the FTA ERP. While similar to the Federal Highway Administration's (FHWA) ERP for highway facilities, the FTA ERP has not received funding on an ongoing basis, which could limit some transit agencies' ability to respond immediately after a disaster. The FHWA ERP is authorized to obligate a specific amount annually to be paid from the Highway Trust Fund,[33] supplemented by appropriations from the General Fund of the U.S. Treasury,[34] on an as-needed basis. While MAP-21 authorized the FTA ERP, Congress, to date, has not provided annual appropriations for the program. The Disaster Relief Appropriations Act, however, provided a one-time appropriation of $10.9 billion for FTA's ERP for recovery, relief, and resilience efforts in areas affected by Hurricane Sandy.[35],[36] Table 2 shows how FTA allocated the ERP funds.

### FTA Technical Assistance Related to Climate Change

The only appropriation that the FTA ERP has received to date is for public transit in areas affected by Hurricane Sandy.[37] Since Sandy, there have been other catastrophic weather-related events, such as mudslides and heavy snow storms. However, Congress did not appropriate ERP funds for those events. If Congress does not appropriate ERP funds for a specific event, transit agencies can still apply through their states for FEMA's assistance and mitigation programs or use their FTA's formula funds. As we discuss below, FTA and transit agency officials told us that demand for limited funds makes it difficult for transit agencies to prioritize actions for building resilience versus other, more immediate needs, such as maintaining and operating existing assets.

**Table 2. Allocation of the $10.2 Billion Disaster Relief Program
Appropriation for the FTA Emergency Relief Program Appropriations,
as of November 2014**

| Notice | Description of allocations |
|---|---|
| March 29, 2013 | $2 billion for response and recovery expenses for Sandyaffected transit agencies |
| May 29, 2013 | $3.7 billion for response, recovery, and local priority resilience funding |
| September 22, 2014 | Approximately $3.6 billion to help transit agencies in Sandyaffected areas become more resilient (e.g., seawall construction and replacement of a deteriorated drawbridge) |
| Not yet announced or allocated | $0.82 billion for remaining unfunded recovery expenses incurred by affected agencies |

Source: GAO analysis of FTA data. | GAO-15-159.

Note: The $10.9 billion appropriations was decreased by 5 percent as a result of the sequestration mandated by the Budget Control Act of 2011 (Pub. L. No. 112-25, 125 Stat. 240 (2011)) and after intergovernmental transfers to other bureaus and offices within DOT.

In May 2011, FTA issued a Policy Statement on Climate Change Adaptation and announced a Climate Change Adaptation initiative. initiative included funding for seven transit climate- change adaptation-assessment pilot programs for assessing the vulnerability of transit agency assets and services to climate change hazards such as heat waves and flooding to help develop strategies that transit agencies can take to mitigate or adapt their systems to better address climate change impacts. DOT expects to issue these projects' final reports in fall 2014. These reports can be a tool, highlighting practices that transit agencies could adopt for their systems. The reports are intended to inform climate change efforts of participating transit agencies and provide information on the efforts' applicability to other transit agencies. In addition, in 2011, FTA issued a study, *Flooded Bus Barns and Buckled Rails*, which it has disseminated to the nation's transit agencies. This study focused on how transit agencies could incorporate climate change adaptation into their systems and activities—such as asset management systems, planning, and emergency response—and provided examples of strategies. In 2011 and 2012, FTA offered workshops for transit agencies on how they can adapt their transit systems so that they are more resilient to the long-term effects of climate change. Further, FTA has held training sessions and workshops for transit agencies to share lessons learned and best practices.

FTA has also funded the Transportation Research Board (TRB) to undertake a research project entitled *Improving the Resiliency of Transit Systems Threatened by Natural Disaster*. Objectives include reviewing current research and developing guidelines, strategies and tools for public transit agencies to make their systems more resilient to natural disasters and climatic events. TRB plans to issue all this work by mid-2016.

### *Other FTA Guidance, Technical Assistance, and Proposed Rulemaking*

In addition to workshops, webinars, and other workgroups sponsored by the American Public Transportation Associations, FTA has held as part of the Climate Change Adaptation initiative, FTA provides guidance and training that can aid transit agencies in preparing for, responding to and mitigating the potential impact of disasters, thereby improving their systems' resilience to such disasters. For example,

- Built-in Redundancy: FTA encourages transit agencies to "build in" redundancy in, among other things, infrastructure, communications, and power supplies.[39] Redundancy of assets and operations within a transit system may help a system respond to catastrophic events by allowing transit agencies to fall back to secondary options rather than ceasing service if a portion of the system is damaged during a disaster.
- Mutual Aid Agreements: FTA recommends—in its guidance—that transit agencies develop mutual aid agreements or memorandums of understanding (MOU) with other relevant organizations and agencies in the same or adjoining communities or areas to, among other things, formalize and authorize assistance during emergencies, so that they can quickly recover and resume operations following a disaster.[40]
- Capital investment decision making: MAP-21[41] requires FTA to develop a transit asset- management system that would, in part, assist transit agencies in prioritizing rehabilitation and replacement investments. These rehabilitation and replacement projects may help transit agencies mitigate the impacts of catastrophic events by incorporating strategies such as elevating assets above flood levels. FTA's October 2013 *Advance Notice of Proposed Rulemaking* on a national transit asset-management system would require transit agencies to, among other things, develop transit asset- management plans to help them make these investment decisions.[42] In a 2013 report, we found that asset management planning is a leading practice

that can help transit agencies plan and prioritize replacement and rehabilitation investments.[43]

## SELECTED TRANSIT AGENCIES TAKE A VARIETY OF ACTIONS TO MAKE THEIR TRANSIT SYSTEMS RESILIENT

Officials from eight of the nine transit agencies we visited told us that they would consider their transit systems to be resilient if they can resist or minimize damage, continue operations, or resume operations quickly, if an emergency were to occur.[44] The transit agencies also identified a number of actions that help improve their systems' resilience, including actions that help them prepare for, respond to, recover from, and mitigate the impacts of emergencies and catastrophic events. These actions include, but are not limited to, developing plans, performing risk assessments, ensuring the continuity of transit system operations, and mitigating the impact of catastrophic events on physical assets.[45]

### Transit Agencies Develop Plans and Perform Risk Assessments

All nine transit agencies have developed plans to help make their systems resilient to catastrophic events. In general, plans can help transit agencies prepare for, respond to, and recover from for catastrophic events should they occur. The plans from the transit agencies that we reviewed can generally be categorized as those that address all-hazards or those that address a specific hazard relevant for transit agencies' locations (see table 3). Transit agencies typically have multiple plans, some of which are described in the table below.

**Table 3. Examples of Plans That Transit Agencies Use to Address Transit System Resilience**

| Type of plan | Examples of plans from selected transit agencies |
|---|---|
| All-hazards plans | • Continuity of operations plans: Eight of the nine[a] selected transit agencies have continuity-of-operations plans. The continuity-of- operations plans that we reviewed describe how the agency will sustain its essential services across a wide range of potential emergencies.<br><br>• Emergency-operations, management, or preparedness plans: All of the selected transit agencies have emergency- |

| Type of plan | Examples of plans from selected transit agencies |
|---|---|
|  | operations, management, or preparedness plans. The plans that we reviewed, among other things, identify the roles and responsibilities of key personnel and describe operational procedures and protocols following an emergency. |
| Hazard-specific plans | • Hurricane plan: Miami-Dade Transit has a plan that prepares the agency for hurricanes. This plan identifies the roles and responsibilities of personnel in the event of a hurricane, describes operational procedures and protocols for emergency services, identifies asset protection strategies, and provides guidance on "return to operations" procedures.<br><br>• Landslide mitigation action plan: Seattle/Puget Sound Region's Sound Transit participated in the development of a plan that describes strategies, such as building retaining walls, to mitigate the impact of landslides along portions of a railroad that are used by Sound Transit's commuter trains. To develop this plan, Sound Transit worked with the Washington State Department of Transportation, Amtrak, and other stakeholders to identify factors of landslides and impacts to passenger rail services. |

Source: GAO summary of information provided by selected transit agencies. I GAO-15-159.

[a] The remaining transit agency is in the process of developing its continuity of operations plan.

All nine transit agencies perform assessments to identify risks to their transit systems so that they can make informed decisions to mitigate the risks and improve resilience. For example, Philadelphia's SEPTA performs a six-stage risk assessment on all of its transit stations. As a part of this assessment, SEPTA police determine the overall rating of stations based on threats, vulnerabilities, and the value of the station to the overall transit system. The agency then develops countermeasure reports that provide recommendations to address identified risks. In addition to developing recommendations to address risks, officials from some transit agencies explained that they use the risk assessments to, among other things, inform the types of training and drills the agencies conduct, or guide their investment decision-making. For example, officials from Seattle/Puget Sound Region's Washington State Ferries told us that one risk area they identified based on a risk assessment of vessels and terminals was that many employees and passengers could sustain injuries during an emergency. As a result, the agency held training to address this risk. Officials from the Los Angeles County Metropolitan Transportation Authority told us they conducted risk assessments to identify areas susceptible to mudslides and as a result, decided to fund the building of retaining walls and fences to stop debris from falling on to the rights-of-way in those areas. Further, based on their risk assessments, officials from Seattle/Puget Sound Region's King County Metro Transit and the Los Angeles County Metropolitan Transportation Authority told us that they identified security risks to their transit tunnels and, as a result, funded actions to enhance security in those tunnels.

In certain instances, transit agencies may not be able to implement solutions to address identified risks because, according to transit officials, funding may be limited, the public or labor unions may disapprove of the suggested solution, or the suggested solution may be cost prohibitive. In such situations, some officials from agencies said that they temporarily accept the risk until better or more cost-effective alternatives are available, or use existing solutions, to address the risks. For example, an official from Miami-Dade Transit explained that when funding is not available to address security risks, the agency's security program supervisors work with facilities maintenance staff to determine whether corrective measures could be addressed during facilities maintenance work.

## Transit Agencies Take Actions to Help Ensure the Continuity of Transit Systems and to Mitigate the Impact of Catastrophic Events on Physical Assets

In addition to developing plans and performing risk assessments, all nine transit agencies showed us or told us about redundant facilities or transit assets to help ensure continuity of transit service if a portion of their systems or facilities is damaged during catastrophic events. For example:

- Six transit agencies have built, are building, or have requested funding to build backup command, control, or communications centers to direct transit operations in case the main center is affected by a catastrophic event. Some of these centers are mobile in nature so that they can change their location as needed. In general, redundant or backup centers provide transit agencies the ability to dispatch trains and buses should the main centers be unable to do so. See Fig. 3.

Source: Orange County Transportation authority.| GAO-15-159.

Figure 3. Mobile Communications Center Used by the Los Angeles Area's Orange County Transportation Authority.

- Los Angeles area's Orange County Transportation Authority uses buses powered by natural gas to provide bus service, but this agency also maintains a small contingency fleet of diesel-powered buses in ready condition that can be placed into service immediately in an emergency. An official from this agency said that this diesel-powered fleet is a critical resource: if a major earthquake, for example, interrupts the delivery of natural gas to his location, the diesel buses could become the only emergency transportation resource capable of being refueled and providing bus service.

- Seattle/Puget Sound Region's Washington State Ferries has ferry terminals that are susceptible to damage during an earthquake. As such, to ensure that ferry service can continue in the event of an emergency, this agency has built terminals with more than one berth to increase the chances that at least one berth will remain functional to some level following a major earthquake. See figure 4 for a terminal with three redundant berths. In addition to redundant berths at any given terminal, Washington State Ferries also has additional terminals that could be used should all the berths at a terminal be unusable. An official from Washington State Ferries said that ensuring the continuity of service for the ferries is important in his region because the ferry system could experience an increase in the number of users while the road systems are being repaired.

Source: GAO.| GAO-15-159.

Figure 4. Three Redundant Berths at Seattle/Puget Sound Region's Washington State Ferries Ferry Terminal.

All nine transit agencies provided us with information about, or told us about, their efforts to coordinate with other local or regional agencies to, for example, help prepare for, respond to, and recover from catastrophic events and to help ensure that their systems can resume or continue operations if such events were to occur. We found transit agencies that have, as FTA suggests, formal agreements with other transit or transportation agencies to facilitate the coordination, and other transit agencies that participate in local or regional transit coordination groups. For example, the Seattle/Puget Sound region's King County Metro Transit has a memorandum of understanding with the City of Seattle's Department of Transportation which defines and coordinates the actions each agency will take during snow events (such as providing certain bus services and removing snow on roads). Additionally, two transit agencies we visited in the Los Angeles region have a formal agreement with other transit agencies in California that describes how transit agencies in the state will, in an emergency, receive and provide mutual assistance to each other in the form of personnel, services, and equipment so that transit systems can continue to operate. Separately, officials from Philadelphia's SEPTA told us that while they do not have a formal agreement with other local transit agencies, they participate in a regional transit working group to, among other things, address common security-related issues, coordinate drills and training, and efficiently administer and procure certain security equipment and other services.

While we did not assess the effectiveness of the selected transit agencies' coordination efforts with other state and local agencies, our July 2009 report on disaster assistance stated that stakeholders faced obstacles with coordination and collaboration after the 2005 Gulf Coast hurricanes.[46] Based on our review of five past disasters, we found that collaborative practices could help communities recover and rebuild from catastrophic events.[47] Accordingly, we recommended that FEMA establish a mechanism for sharing information and best practices focused on disaster recovery, including practices that promote effective collaboration. In September 2013, we found that FEMA had implemented this recommendation.

In addition, eight transit agencies we visited showed or told us about changes they have made to their physical infrastructure to mitigate the impacts of catastrophic events on their transit systems. For example:

- Miami-Dade Transit made changes to better protect its electrified third rail and reduce damage and replacement costs. This transit agency uses cover boards to protect the electrified third rail that supply power to its trains. Officials from this transit agency told us that hurricane winds ripped off cover boards in some places, damage that prompted them to look for better solutions to protect the third rail. As a result, officials installed newly designed cover boards that allow winds to flow through the cover, rather than catch the wind—thus allowing the cover boards and the third rail to better withstand hurricane winds (see fig. 5.)

Source: GAO. | GAO-15-159.

Note: Washington State Ferries also has additional terminals that could be used if all berths at a terminal become unusable.

Figure 5. Miami-Dade Transit's Cover Boards for the Third Rail: Old Design Can Be Blown Off by High Winds (Left), and New Design Mitigates Wind Damage (Right).

- Philadelphia's SEPTA changed its roadside curbs and subway vents to reduce subway flooding. Flooding is one of the key risks to this transit agency's rail system. Officials explained that subway flooding occurs, in part, because water accumulates near roadside curbs that have deteriorated, thus allowing water to enter vents that provide air to the underground train system. To remedy the problem, the transit agency raised curbs or vents throughout the city to minimize water flow into the vents (see fig. 6). Prior to implementing this renovation, the transit agency had previously relied on a strategy of covering vents susceptible to flooding with plywood and sand bags in advance of large storms, but this process was labor intensive and dependent on how much time was available before a storm.

Source: GAO. | GAO-15-159.

Figure 6. Deteriorated Curb That Allowed Water to Easily Enter Subway (Left) and Raised Curb and Vent That Minimized Water Flow into Subway (Center and Right).

## TRANSIT AGENCIES FACE CHALLENGES IN PLACING PRIORITY ON RESILIENCE AND WITH CERTAIN ASPECTS OF SOME FEDERAL GRANTS

Officials from DOT, DHS, transit agencies and emergency management offices we visited stated that transit agencies face challenges related to placing priority on resilience and some aspects of certain grant programs that can help make transit systems resilient.[48] These challenges were the most frequently cited challenges across the agencies we reviewed.[49,50] DOT, DHS, and some transit agencies have taken or are taking some actions to address identified challenges.

## Placing Priority on Resilience May Be Challenging

Officials from DOT, DHS, and the transit agencies and emergency management offices we visited identified a variety of challenges that make it difficult for transit agencies to place priority on resilience activities.

First, officials from DOT and DHS told us that resilience may not be a priority for transit agency managers. These managers may not make resilience a priority because it is difficult for them to make the case for resilience projects and because catastrophic events occur infrequently. As far back as June 1998, we reported that state and local governments might be reluctant to take actions that improve resilience to natural hazards because, among other reasons, decision-makers may not have complete or accurate information on the extent to which averted losses could exceed the increased cost of resilience actions.[51] Gathering comprehensive and reliable data to make decisions about cost-benefit tradeoffs continues to be difficult. FTA has developed a tool to help transit agencies in Sandy-affected areas evaluate the cost-effectiveness of resilience projects in reducing the vulnerabilities of both an asset and of the public transportation system to future disasters. This information on cost-effectiveness was among the factors FTA used to help it determine which resilience projects would receive ERP funds. Additionally, three transit researchers whom we interviewed agreed that it can be challenging to convince management that preparing transit systems for future catastrophic events should be a priority; they further explained that this is because such events may not happen or may happen infrequently.

Second, officials from four transit agencies we visited as well as DOT, and DHS indicated that resilience activities compete with other priorities for funding.

- *Competing with other transit agency priorities:* Resilience activities may compete with other transit agency priorities—such as those that address systems operations —for funding. For example, an official from Seattle/Puget Sound Region's Washington State Ferries explained that because his transit system lost a critical source of funding—the state's motor-vehicle excise tax—the agency needed to direct its existing funding sources to operating and construction costs, which left little room for resilience-related activities, such as building redundant systems. Officials from Philadelphia's SEPTA told us that they sometimes have to prioritize funding to address federal requirements—such as a requirement to install positive train control on railroads used to transport commuters, inter-city rail passengers, or hazardous materials—which limits the funding that is available for other agency activities such as those that help make their system resilient.[52]

- *Competing with other state priorities:* In 1998, 2007, and 2014, we found that state and local governments might be reluctant to invest in resilience-building activities—such as hazard mitigation—because leaders may be concerned that these activities will detract from economic development goals that may be a higher priority for communities.[53] According to a FEMA official, transit systems have not been high priority in states' applications for FEMA mitigation grants, such as the HMGP, in part because states tend to focus on other priorities that are of interest to communities. The FEMA official told us, for example, that after Hurricane Sandy, a state prioritized HMGP grants for residential housing rather than for transit. An official from an emergency management office said that these competing priorities may limit the funding provided to transit agencies and affect their ability to undertake activities that could help make their systems resilient.

Third, officials from seven transit agencies and four emergency-management offices said that federal funds are not always available for transit systems' resilience and limits their ability to undertake activities that could help make their systems resilient. Officials from some of these transit agencies said that federal funds are not always available to help them make their systems resilient to catastrophic events, particularly natural disasters, before they occur. For example, as discussed earlier, ERP funds are currently available only after an event occurs and only if Congress provides an appropriation specific to the event. Furthermore, according to officials from one transit agency and two emergency management offices, federal funds provided after a disaster to improve resilience to future disasters are limited. An official from the transit agency said that funding is limited because federal funds provided after a disaster, other than through the ERP, are largely focused on recovery and not mitigation or other activities that can be used to address resilience. An official from one of the two emergency management offices said that following a disaster, state or local funding may not be readily available to cover the federal cost sharing requirements applicable to federally funded projects, thus preventing them from receiving the federal funds. In addition, officials from some of the transit agencies said that funding for the TSGP, a grant program that helps transit agencies improve their systems' resilience to security risks, is sporadic and difficult to obtain or has declined. As discussed earlier, TSGP funds for public transit peaked in fiscal year 2009 at almost $500 million; but were at or below $90 million in each of the past 3 fiscal years. Miami-Dade Transit officials said that the lack of TSGP funding has made it difficult to obtain funding to implement security upgrades at facilities, and officials from Seattle/Puget Sound Region's King County Metro Transit said the decline has made it difficult to obtain funds to maintain implemented security solutions.[54] The four transit researchers we spoke with agreed that the availability of funds for resilience is a challenge for transit agencies. Two of these transit researchers further explained that funding resilience activities is especially challenging for smaller transit agencies or agencies that do not have enough funding from fare box revenue to address their operating costs.

Making choices about how to prioritize activities given finite resources is not a new or unique dilemma for transit agencies. In March 2006, we found that while transit agencies that operate rail systems may use FTA financial assistance for security activities, such as upgrading security technologies, they must balance and prioritize such investments in security against other competing needs.[55] Furthermore, making choices about how to prioritize activities, which involves the consideration of trade-offs, is similar to the process that other organizations, including Congress and federal agencies, must go through when confronted with funding requests that have merit, but exceed the amount of available funding.[56] Nonetheless, as noted below, some stakeholders we interviewed are considering actions to assist transit agencies place priority on resilience activities.

Philadelphia's SEPTA and FTA are considering some actions that could help place priorities on resilience activities within their agency:

- While participating in an FTA-funded climate-change adaptation-assessment pilot program, officials from SEPTA found, that one strategy that could help ensure that the agency addresses resilience across a range of weather events is to incorporate assets' climate change vulnerabilities in SEPTA's asset management program. The 2013 report that summarized the results of the pilot program concluded that if this vulnerability information is included in an asset management program, decision-makers can use this information to help them determine how to address those issues in future maintenance or new construction investments.[57] This agency has incorporated elements of this strategy into its asset management program.

- FTA issued an *Advance Notice of Proposed Rulemaking* on an asset management system, as discussed earlier, and is considering whether risk analyses, among other things, should be included in transit agencies' asset management plans to help transit agencies make investment and other decisions. [58]While the proposed rulemaking does not specifically refer to transit system resilience, consideration of a transit system's risk during investment prioritization decisions could help minimize those risks and thus improve the resilience of a system.

## Some Federal Grant Program Requirements Pose Challenges for Use of Federal Funds for Resilience

Transit agency, emergency management, and federal officials also cited challenges specifically related to some aspects of federal grants, challenges that have affected how or the extent to which transit system resilience is addressed. These challenges are discussed below.

- *Incorporating resilience into disaster recovery:* Officials from emergency management offices in Miami-Dade County and Philadelphia as well as officials from Philadelphia's SEPTA and a FEMA official, identified challenges with incorporating mitigation activities into disaster recovery due to the difficulty of coordinating available funding streams. As discussed above, mitigation is one action that can contribute to resilience. After a presidentially declared major disaster or emergency, an affected state can request funds from FEMA's Public Assistance grant program for response and recovery efforts, such as for repairing or replacing disaster-damaged transportation infrastructure.[59] However, an official from one of the emergency management offices said that because federal and state processes for distributing federal funds that can be used for mitigation (i.e., FEMA's Hazard Mitigation Grant Program funds) takes time, transit agencies may not be able to use these funds during their recovery efforts, such as those that occur with the help of the Public Assistance grants. Further, an official from another emergency management office said that hazard mitigation grants become available after much of the rebuilding is under way or complete. Given the different timelines for the Public Assistance and Hazard Mitigation Grants, opportunities to incorporate resilience into projects occurring during the recovery stages of a disaster can be missed. Determining when agencies should focus on resilience and recovery can be difficult. In March 2010, we found that state and local governments might not have the capacity to focus on recovery soon after a disaster.[60] We have ongoing work to evaluate select efforts to facilitate resilience as part of the Sandy recovery effort. We plan to issue a report on these efforts in 2015.

- *Decreased focus on regional resilience.* Officials from Philadelphia's SEPTA, the Los Angeles area's Orange County Transportation Authority, the Los Angeles County Metropolitan Transportation Authority, and one emergency management office said that changes with FEMA's TSGP grant program has affected efforts to improve regional resilience. In fiscal year 2011, DHS revised its policy for the TSGP grant program from one where the funds were allocated to high-risk regions and given to transit agencies in those regions using a collaborative process to a nationally competitive grant program where all transit agencies nationwide competed for the funds. When grants were regionally allocated, transit agencies were required to work together to determine how best to request and allocate TSGP funds for their region. According to officials from two transit agencies, such collaboration with other transit agencies in their region is important because a city's transit network is often comprised of transit systems run by multiple transit agencies. However, when the grant program became competitive, officials from three transit agencies and one emergency-management office said that transit agencies had less incentive to collaborate with other transit agencies in their region because all the agencies were competing for the same pool of TSGP funds. FEMA officials told us that the grant program still encourages regional collaboration because such collaboration is a criterion for determining grant distributions. Furthermore, one emergency-management office said that changes with another FEMA grant program—the Regional Catastrophic Preparedness Grant Program—also potentially limited regional coordination. In fiscal year 2012, the

Regional Catastrophic Preparedness Grant Program—which was used to support regional all-hazard planning for catastrophic events— was discontinued as it was no longer funded. According to FEMA officials, this grant program enabled agencies, including transit agencies, in a region to coordinate their preparedness and planning efforts with other agencies in their region. However, officials from the emergency management office told us that the discontinuance of the grant program may limit transit agency coordination and cooperation that existed under the grant as agencies compete with one another for other FEMA preparedness grants. Despite transit agencies' decreased incentive to coordinate with other transit agencies, we found—as we discuss earlier—that transit agencies continue to coordinate with other transit agencies through formal agreements or by participating in local or regional transit coordination groups.

- *Short period of performance to address resilience of certain assets:* In fiscal year 2012, DHS changed the period of performance for the TSGP grants from 3 to 4 years— depending on the type of project—to 2 years. According to DHS officials, DHS took this action to encourage transit agencies to use their grants quickly. Officials from Philadelphia's SEPTA told us that DHS's requirement that transit agencies complete projects funded by TSGP grants in 2 years makes it challenging for their agency to undertake projects that address resilience. Specifically, these officials explained that because of DHS's emphasis on completing projects within 2 years, transit agencies cannot fully address the resilience of the assets needing greater attention because projects related to these assets generally take longer than 2 years to complete. According to DHS officials, based on a review of seven transit agencies, the length of time for completing transit security projects that require construction ranged from about 2.5 to about 5 years, depending on the type of project.61 Transit agencies may request an extension to the 2-year period of performance; however, according to DHS guidance on the grants, such extensions are only given under exceptional circumstances, such as if a natural disaster or other major event were to occur or if complex environmental reviews cannot be completed within the time frame. A DHS official told us that his agency recognizes the 2-year performance period to be a challenge for transit agencies and said that DHS is working with transit agencies and Congress to find the right balance between getting funding deployed versus the length of time it takes to complete more complex projects. The extent of this challenge may differ depending on each agency's system. For example, a transit researcher we spoke to said that in general, shorter performance periods are typically not a problem for transit agencies that primarily have bus fleets because projects associated with buses do not take as long to complete as rail projects.

## CONCLUDING OBSERVATIONS

One of the goals of public transit systems, post-disaster, is to resume operations as quickly as possible. After catastrophic events, a system can take days, weeks, or months to fully recover and rebuild. In the past 13 years, the vulnerability of transit systems to catastrophic events has been repeatedly demonstrated as these events, particularly extreme weather events, have occurred more frequently. Such events are expected to increase going forward. Given that catastrophic events can be challenging to predict, transit agencies find themselves in the difficult situation of trying to balance the needs of daily operations with preparing for such events. There is a constant need to balance the immediate needs with the "what-if" needs as decision-makers prioritize use of their finite resources. The role of the federal government in providing resilience-related assistance to transit agencies may fluctuate, depending on the catastrophic events and the related authority and appropriations Congress provides to DOT and DHS. While it is not possible to make a transit system completely immune to catastrophic events, continued efforts by all parties to place priority on and improve resilience through preparedness, response, recovery, and mitigation can help our nation's transit systems potentially better withstand and recover from such events and reduce their human and economic impacts.

## AGENCY COMMENTS

We provided DHS and DOT with a draft of this report for review and comment. DHS and DOT provided technical comments, which we incorporated in the report as appropriate.

David J. Wise, Director, Physical Infrastructure

# APPENDIX I: OBJECTIVES, SCOPE, AND METHODOLOGY

This report examines (1) how DOT and DHS help transit agencies make their systems resilient to catastrophic events; (2) actions selected transit agencies take to make their systems resilient; and (3) challenges transit agencies face with making their systems resilient to such events. Catastrophic events are those that result in extraordinary levels of mass casualties, damage, or disruption severely affecting the population, infrastructure, environment, economy, national morale, and/or government functions. Our review focuses on catastrophic events caused either by nature (e.g., hurricanes, flooding, fires) or by humans (e.g., security events, including terrorism). Transit modes included in our review include rail transit (light-rail, heavy rail, commuter rail), bus, and ferry systems.

To determine the activities DOT and DHS take to help transit agencies make their systems resilient to catastrophic events, we reviewed and analyzed documentation from the two federal agencies on their relevant funding programs, requirements, guidance, policies, and technical assistance.[1] We also interviewed officials from these two agencies. In addition, we reviewed funding data from DHS for the Transit Security Grant Program from fiscal years 2005 through 2014 and assessed the reliability of the data by interviewing agency officials. We determined that the data were reliable for the purposes of describing the amount of funding awarded for public transit. Also, to understand the federal government's overall approach to addressing resilience, we reviewed Executive Orders, Presidential Policy Directives, Homeland Security Presidential Directives, and national policy statements or plans for national critical infrastructure protection and climate change adaptation. Furthermore, we interviewed officials from transit agencies and emergency management offices in five metropolitan areas for their observations on DOT and DHS assistance. The five selected areas and the criteria we used to select them are described below.

To identify actions selected transit agencies take to make their systems resilient, we reviewed documentation and interviewed officials from nine transit agencies and five local emergency management offices in five metropolitan areas (see table 4).[2] The five selected areas are Los Angeles, California; Miami, Florida; Philadelphia, Pennsylvania; Seattle/Puget Sound Region, Washington; and Washington, D.C. We selected the five metropolitan areas because they (1) are located in different geographic areas and have the potential exposure to different types of weather- and non-weather related risks (e.g., hurricanes, earthquakes, terrorism), (2) have varying types of transit modes (light-rail, heavy rail, commuter rail, bus, and ferry), and (3) are among the 10 largest metropolitan areas in terms of transit ridership.3 While we did not interview all transit agencies in each metropolitan area, we selected those that had relatively high transit ridership, were located in the city, or provided service to the city. While the information we obtained from the five areas is not generalizable to transit systems nationwide, the selected areas have some of the larger transit systems in terms of ridership. When we report the number of agencies that took a particular action to make their systems resilient, this does not necessarily mean that the remaining agencies did not also take those actions. It means that those agencies did not discuss those actions in documents provided to us or during the course of our interviews.

**Table 4. Emergency Management Offices and Transit Agencies Selected for GAO's Review**

| Metropolitan area | Selected emergency management office | Selected transit agency |
|---|---|---|
| Los Angeles, California | Los Angeles Operational Area Critical Incident Planning and Training Alliance, whose core members are the Los Angeles Sheriff's, Police, and Fire Departments; the Los Angeles County Fire Department and Office of Emergency Management; and the Red Cross. The Los Angeles County Metropolitan Transportation Authority participates in this Alliance. | Los Angeles County Metropolitan Transportation Authority |
| | | Orange County Transportation Authority |
| | | Southern California Regional Rail Authority (Metrolink) |
| Miami, Florida | Miami-Dade's Office of Emergency Management, a Division of Miami-Dade Fire Rescue | Miami-Dade Transit |
| Philadelphia, Pennsylvania | Philadelphia Office of Emergency Management | Southeastern Pennsylvania Transportation Authority (SEPTA) |
| Seattle/Puget Sound Region, Washington | City of Seattle Office of Emergency Management | Washington State Ferries |
| | | King County Metro Transit |

**Table 4. (Continued)**

| Metropolitan area | Selected emergency management office | Selected transit agency |
|---|---|---|
|  |  | Sound Transit |
| Washington, D.C. | District of Columbia Homeland Security and Emergency Management Agency | Washington Metropolitan Area Transit Authority (WMATA) |

Sources: GAO I GAO-15-159.

Note: In each metropolitan area, we selected transit agencies that were located in the city itself or provided service to the city. Also, we selected transit agencies that had relatively high ridership.

To identify challenges transit agencies face with making their systems resilient to catastrophic events, we asked officials from DOT, DHS, the nine transit agencies, and five emergency management offices to identify challenges. Officials identified challenges when we explicitly asked them to identify them or during the course of our discussion. We analyzed the information gained from these officials to identify the most frequently cited challenges. The most frequently cited challenges were those that were cited by four or more transit agencies (about half of the transit agencies selected), two or more emergency management offices (about half of the emergency management offices selected), or both DOT and DHS. When we report the number of agencies that identified a particular challenge, this does not necessarily mean that the remaining agencies did not also experience the challenge. It means that those stakeholders did not raise the challenge during the course of our interviews. We also interviewed four researchers knowledgeable in transit systems, emergency management, or federal transportation programs to further understand the challenges transit agencies face. We identified these researchers based on our review of transportation research institutes and recommendations from officials we interviewed.

We conducted this performance audit from October 2013 through December 2014 in accordance with generally accepted government auditing standards. Those standards require that we plan and perform the audit to obtain sufficient, appropriate evidence to provide a reasonable basis for our findings and conclusions based on our audit objectives. We believe that the evidence obtained provides a reasonable basis for our findings and conclusions on our audit objectives.

# End Notes

[1] According to the Department of Homeland Security, catastrophic events are emergencies or disasters that result in extraordinary levels of mass casualties, damage, or disruption severely affecting the population, infrastructure, environment, economy, national morale, and/or government functions.

[2] Sandy has been referred as both a hurricane and a "Superstorm." The National Hurricane Center declared Sandy a hurricane, but changed that designation to "post-tropical" storm just before it made landfall. In this report, we refer to the event as "Hurricane Sandy."

[3] Disaster Relief Appropriations Act (DRAA), 2013, Pub. L. No. 113-2, div. A, 127 Stat. 4 (2013). These amounts are not adjusted to account for sequestration under section 251A of the Balanced Budget and Emergency Deficit Control Act of 1985, as amended, which the Office of Management and Budget calculated would amount to a 5 percent reduction in nonexempt, nondefense discretionary funding for the fiscal year.

[4] "The Federal Transit Administration (FTA), under its Emergency Relief Program, defines 'resilience' as 'the ability to anticipate, prepare for, and adapt to changing conditions and withstand, respond to, and recover rapidly from disruptions such as significant multi-hazard threats with minimum damage to social well-being, the economy, and the environment." FTA defines a 'resilience project' as "a project designed and built to address existing and future vulnerabilities to a public transportation facility or system due to a probable occurrence or recurrence of an emergency or major disaster in the geographic area in which the public transportation system is located, and which may include the consideration of projected changes in development patterns, demographics, or climate change and extreme weather patterns." 49 C.F.R. § 602.5.

[5] The U.S. Global Change Research Program was established by Presidential Initiative in 1989 and mandated by Congress in the Global Change Research Act of 1990, Pub. L. No. 101-606, 104 Stat. 3096 (1990), to "assist the Nation and the world to understand, assess, predict, and respond to human-induced and natural processes of global change.

[6] Because the impacts of these events will result in increased fiscal exposure for the federal government in many areas, including critical transportation, we placed limiting fiscal exposure from climate change on our High Risk list. See GAO-13-283, High-Risk Series: An Update (Washington, D.C.: February 2013)

[7] According DHS, mitigation is the effort to reduce loss of life and property by lessening the impact of disasters.

[8] See for example GAO, Disaster Resilience: Actions Are Underway, but Federal Fiscal Exposure Highlights the Need for Continued Attention to Longstanding Challenges, GAO-14-603T (Washington, D.C.: May 14, 2014) and GAO, Climate Change: Future Federal Adaptation Efforts Could Better Support Local Infrastructure Decision Makers, GAO-13-242 (Washington, D.C.: Apr. 12, 2013).

[9] See GAO-14-512 and GAO-14-603T.

[10] The U.S. Coast Guard has responsibilities over the security of ferry systems. We did not include the Coast Guard in the scope of our study.

[11] Ridership is based on FTA's 2011 National Transit Database's total unlinked passenger trips. Total unlinked passenger trips are the number of passengers who board public transportation vehicles. Passengers are counted each time they board vehicles no matter how many vehicles they use to travel from their origin to their destination.

[12] The other 15 critical infrastructure sectors are chemical; commercial facilities; communications; critical manufacturing; dams; defense industrial base; emergency services;

energy; financial services; food and agriculture; government facilities; healthcare and public health; information technology; nuclear reactors, materials, and waste; and water and wastewater systems.

[13] Resilience can incorporate a number of activities, such as engaging the whole community in the planning phase, linking public and private infrastructure interests, and communicating risks throughout the community.

[14] Pub. L. No. 100-707, 102 Stat. 4689 (1988). Robert T. Stafford Disaster Relief and Emergency Assistance Act, as amended, constitutes the statutory authority for federal disaster response activities especially as they pertain to FEMA and FEMA programs.

[15] In addition to FEMA's mitigation funds, communities may be able to seek recovery funds for resilience projects from other federal agencies, including the Department of Housing and Urban Development's Community Development Block Grant (CDBG) funds. CDBG funds are allocated to states by formula.

[16] After the establishment of DHS by the Homeland Security Act of 2002, Pub. L. No. 107- 296, 116 Stat 2135 (2002), oversight of public transit systems' security was transferred from DOT to DHS. The two departments have signed a memorandum of understanding to clarify their respective authorities over public transit systems and to provide departmental coordination.

[17] Sections 1405 (6 U.S.C. § 1134) and 1406 (6 U.S.C. § 1135) of the Implementing Regulations of the 9/11 Commission Act of 2007 (9-11 Act), Pub. L. No. 110-53, 121 Stat. 266, 402 (2007).

[18] 49 U.S.C. § 5307 (Urbanized areas), § 5310 (Formula Grants for the enhanced mobility of seniors and individuals with disabilities), § 5311 (non-urbanized areas), § 5337 (State of Good Repair Grants), §§ 5339 (and 5324) (Bus and Bus Facilities Formula Grants).Discretionary grants are authorized under 49 U.S.C. § 5309.

[19] Formula grants are allocated based on formulas prescribed in statute or regulation. Discretionary grants are generally awarded on a competitive basis to eligible applicants for specific projects.

[20] Funds under §§ 5307, 5311 (and 5324) are eligible to be used for operating expenses.

[21] According to TSA officials, the BASE is a voluntary assessment; that is, it is an assessment used by TSA to encourage transit agency implementation of requirements, guidance, and standards—not to enforce compliance. TSA focuses BASE assessments on the nation's top 100 transit systems, as identified by FTA, based on ridership and revenues.

[22] Sections 1405 and 1406 of the Implementing Regulations of the 9/11 Commission Act of 2007, Pub. L. No. 110-53, 121 Stat. 266, 402 (2007), codified at 6 U.S.C. § 1134 and 6 U.S.C. § 1135, respectively.

[23] Prior to fiscal year 2012, FEMA typically required transit agencies to use their TSGP funds within 3 to 4 years. However, FEMA found that transit agencies were taking too long to use their grants, thus resulting in large balances of unused funds. As a result, in fiscal year 2012, DHS changed the period of performance for the TSGP grants to 2 years to encourage transit agencies to use their grants quickly.

[24] TSGP funds awarded for public transit were made available through annual appropriations, starting in fiscal year 2005. Funds were also provided through a supplemental appropriation in fiscal year 2007, and the American Recovery and Reinvestment Act of 2009 in fiscal year 2009.

25 According to a FEMA official, FTA is invited to be part of this panel and has participated in some years, depending on availability of FTA staff.

[26] According to FEMA officials, to get information about how these funds were used by transit agencies, they would need to ask the states for the information. While FEMA tracks information on the funds at the state level, it does not track how states disseminate funds among all their sub-grantees.

[27] In March 2010, we found that some federal recovery funds after Hurricane Ike in 2007 and the Midwest floods in 2008 were released shortly after the disasters, making it challenging for some state and local governments to focus on recovery because they had limited capacity to do so at that time. In that report, we recommended that DHS, among other things, establish a long-term recovery structure to more effectively align the timing and level of involvement of the entity responsible for coordinating long-term community recovery assistance with the capacity of the affected state and local governments. See GAO, Disaster Recovery: FEMA's Long-term Assistance Was Helpful to State and Local Governments but Had Some Limitation, GAO-10-404 (Washington, D.C.: Mar. 30, 2010). In September 2011, FEMA issued the National Disaster Recovery Framework, which established a recovery structure intended to more effectively align the timing and level of long-term community recovery assistance with the capacity of state and local governments. In early 2015, GAO will issue a report that will evaluate whether Hurricane Sandy-affected areas are incorporating resilience into recovery efforts, and the challenges stakeholders in these areas experience.

[28] FTA defines a rail "fixed guideway system" as any light, heavy, or rapid rail system, monorail, inclined plane, funicular, trolley, or automated guideway that: (1) is not regulated by the Federal Railway Administration; and (2) is included in FTA's calculation of fixed guideway route miles, or receives funding under FTA's formula programs for urbanized areas; or (3) has submitted documentation to FTA indicating its intent to be included in FTA's calculation of fixed-guideway route miles to receive funding under FTA's formula programs for urbanized areas. 49 C.F.R.§ 659.5.

[29] 49 U.S.C. § 5339.

[30] FTA Circular 5010.1D, Grant Management Requirements, (Nov. 1, 2008).

[31] According to FTA officials, FTA does not track how often grantees have been required to return funds if their assets did not last through their useful life.

[32] Pub. L. No. 112-14, § 20017(a), 126 Stat. 405, 703, codified at 49 U.S.C. § 5324.

[33] The Highway Trust Fund is an account established by law to hold federal highway user tax receipts (e.g., receipts for federal excise taxes on fuel and other taxes on commercial trucks) that are dedicated for highway and transit related purposes.

[34] The General Fund of the U.S. Treasury holds federal money not allocated by law to any other fund account.

[35] After the enactment of the Budget Control Act of 2011 (Pub. L. No. 112-25, 125 Stat. 240(2011)), this amount decreased by 5 percent.

[36] See GAO, Emergency Transportation Relief: Agencies Could Improve Collaboration Begun During Hurricane Sandy Response, GAO-14-512 (Washington, D.C.: May 28, 2014) for more information about disaster relief transit agencies affected by Hurricane Sandy.

[37] Pub. L. No. 113-2, div. A, title X, 127 Stat. 4, 35.

[38] This is in response to Executive Orders and DOT's policy statements on climate change.

[39] Research and Special Programs Administration, U.S. Department of Transportation and John A. Volpe National Transportation Systems Center, Transit Security Design Considerations (November 2004); and John A. Volpe National Transportation Systems Center for Intelligent Transportation Systems Joint Program Office, U.S. Department of Transportation, Effects of Catastrophic Events on Transportation System Management and Operations (January 2003).

[40] Federal Transit Administration, Response and Recovery for Declared Emergencies and Disasters: A Resource Document for Transit Agencies (Washington, D.C.: April 2012).

[41] Pub. L. No. 112-141,126 Stat. 405 (2012) authorized surface transportation programs through fiscal year 2014. Legislation was enacted in August 2014 extending surface transportation programs and funding through May 31, 2015, for programs authorized under MAP-21. Highway and Transportation Funding Act, Pub. L. No. 113-159, 128 Stat. 1839 (2014.

[42] 78 Fed. Reg. 61251 (Oct. 3, 2013).

[43] GAO-13-571, Transit Asset Management: Additional Research on Capital Investment Effects Could Help Transit Agencies Optimize Funding (Washington, D.C.: July 11, 2013)

[44] Officials at the remaining transit agency said that they have not adopted a definition for transit system resilience.

[45] When we report the number of agencies that took a particular action to make their systems resilient, this does not necessarily mean that the remaining agencies did not also take those actions. It means that those agencies did not discuss those actions in documents provided to us or during the course of our interviews.

[46] GAO, Disaster Recovery: Experiences from Past Disasters Offer Insights for Effective Collaboration after Catastrophic Events, GAO-09-811 (Washington, D.C.: July 31, 2009).

[47] The five disaster discussed are the Loma Prieta Earthquake, Hurricane Andrew, the Northridge Earthquake, the Kobe Earthquake, and the Grand Forks/Red River Flood. We found that key collaborative practices include (1) developing and communicating common goals to guide recovery, (2) leveraging resources to facilitate recovery, (3) using recovery plans to agree on roles and responsibilities, and (4) monitoring, evaluating, and reporting on progress made toward recovery. See GAO-09-811.

[48] During interviews with officials from DOT, DHS, the nine selected transit agencies, and five selected emergency management offices, officials identified challenges when we explicitly asked them to do so or during the course of our discussion. When we report the number of agencies that identified a particular challenge, this does not necessarily mean that the remaining agencies did not also experience the challenge. It means that those stakeholders did not raise the challenge during the course of our interviews.

[49] The methodology we used to determine the most frequently cited challenges is described in appendix I.

[50] In addition to the challenges frequently identified by agencies we interviewed, we also heard about other challenges, but less frequently, that transit agencies face with making their systems resilient to catastrophic events. These challenges, as identified by transit agencies, include (1) incorporating resilience into transit agency planning or project design; (2) limited ability for smaller transit agencies to address resilience because of their size (such as limited staff and funding resources); (3) limited flexibility in addressing local or transit agency risks; (4) limitations with federal grant requirements (such as a requirement to provide a percentage of non-federal funds to FEMA-funded projects); (5) aging infrastructure; and (6) duplication and redundancy across federal efforts.

[51] GAO, Disaster Assistance: Information on Federal Disaster Mitigation Efforts, GAO/T-RCED-98-67 (Washington D.C.: Jan. 28, 1998).

[52] Positive train control is a communications-based system designed to prevent certain types of accidents caused by human factors, such as train-to-train collisions, trains entering work zones, and derailments. The Rail Safety Improvement Act required that positive train control be installed by December 31, 2015. Pub. L. No. 110-432, div.A, § 104, 122 Stat. 4848, 4856(2008). In August 2013, we found that most railroads said that they would miss the deadline due to numerous challenges caused by the breadth and complexity of installing

the system. See GAO-13-720, Positive Train Control: Additional Authorities Could Benefit Implementation (Washington, D.C., Aug. 16, 2013).

[53] GAO/T-RCED-98-67; GAO, Natural Hazard Mitigation: Various Mitigation Efforts Exist, but Federal Efforts Do Not Provide a Comprehensive Strategic Framework, GAO-07-403 (Washington, D.C.: Aug. 22, 2007); and GAO-14-603T.

[54] Maintaining resilience-related infrastructure improvements and technologies after they have been implemented was another frequently cited challenge by transit agencies, with five transit agencies citing this as a challenge.

[55] GAO, Passenger Rail Security: Evaluating Foreign Security Practices and Risk Can Help Guide Security Efforts, GAO-06-557T (Washington, D.C.: Mar. 29, 2006).

[56] For example, in April 2009, we found that while Congress and federal agencies expressed frustration with the budget and appropriations process, it is in the annual appropriations process that the Congress considers, debates, and makes decisions about the competing claims for federal resources. Congress is confronted every year with claims that have merit but which in total exceed the amount the Congress believes appropriate to spend. It is not an easy process—but it is an important exercise of the constitutional power of the purse. GAO, VA Health Care: Challenges in Budget Formulation and Issues Surrounding the Proposal for Advance Appropriations, GAO-09-664T (Washington, D.C.: Apr. 29, 2009).

[57] ICF International, A Vulnerability and Risk Assessment of SEPTA's Regional Rail: A Transit Climate Change Adaptation Assessment Pilot, a report prepared at the request of the Federal Transit Administration, Department of Transportation (August 2013).

[58] 78 Fed. Reg. 61252 (Oct. 3, 2013).

[59] FTA ERP funds are not available to transit agencies unless Congress provides an appropriation for the ERP, as it did in the aftermath of Hurricane Sandy.

[60] GAO-10-404.

[61] We did not independently verify these time frames.

# End Notes for Appendix I

[1] The U.S. Coast Guard has responsibilities over the security of ferry systems. We did not include the Coast Guard in the scope of our study.

[2] We interviewed officials in-person or over the phone, or obtained responses to our interview questions via email.

[3] Ridership is based on FTA's 2011 National Transit Database's total unlinked passenger trips. Total unlinked passenger trips are the number of passengers who board public transportation vehicles. Passengers are counted each time they board vehicles no matter how many vehicles they use to travel from their origin to their destination.

In: Transit System Resilience        ISBN: 978-1-63482-567-2
Editor: Kayla Hodges        © 2015 Nova Science Publishers, Inc.

*Chapter 2*

# EMERGENCY TRANSPORTATION RELIEF: AGENCIES COULD IMPROVE COLLABORATION BEGUN DURING HURRICANE SANDY RESPONSE*

## *United States Government Accountability Office*

### ABBREVIATIONS

| | |
|---|---|
| CBO | Congressional Budget Office |
| CRS | Congressional Research Service |
| DHS | Department of Homeland Security |
| DOT | Department of Transportation |
| DRAA | Disaster Relief Appropriations Act, 2013 |
| DRF | Disaster Relief Fund |
| FEMA | Federal Emergency Management Agency |
| FHWA | Federal Highway Administration |
| FRA | Federal Railroad Administration |
| FTA | Federal Transit Administration |
| MAP-21 | Moving Ahead for Progress in the 21st Century Act |

---

* This is an edited, reformatted and augmented version of The United States Government Accountability Office publication, GAO-14-512, dated May 2014.

NORTA      New Orleans Regional Transit Authority
OIG        Office of Inspector General

# WHY GAO DID THIS STUDY

In October 2012, Hurricane Sandy devastated portions of the Mid-Atlantic coast causing severe damage to transit facilities and infrastructure and disrupting mobility in the New York metropolitan region. In January 2013, the President signed the DRAA, which provided approximately $50.5 billion in federal aid for expenses related to Hurricane Sandy. GAO was asked to examine DRAA emergency relief assistance for transportation.

This report addresses (1) the progress DOT has made allocating, obligating, and disbursing DRAA surface transportation funds, (2) how FTA's new Public Transportation Emergency Relief program compares to FEMA's and FHWA's emergency relief programs, and (3) the extent to which FTA and FEMA have implemented their memorandum of agreement to coordinate their roles and responsibilities when providing assistance to transit agencies. GAO analyzed relevant laws, regulations, and agency documentation, and interviewed DOT, FEMA, and New Jersey and New York area transit officials.

# WHAT GAO RECOMMENDS

GAO recommends that DOT and the Department of Homeland Security (DHS) direct FTA and FEMA to establish specific guidelines to monitor, evaluate, and report the results of collaborative efforts—including their communications program and protocol as contemplated in their memorandum of agreement. DHS agreed with our recommendation, and DOT took no position. DHS and DOT also provided technical comments, which we incorporated as appropriate.

# WHAT GAO FOUND

The Department of Transportation (DOT) is in the process of allocating, obligating, and disbursing the $13 billion appropriated by the Disaster Relief

Appropriations Act, 2013 (DRAA) for surface transportation relief. Most of the DRAA surface transportation funds—over $10 billion—were appropriated to the Federal Transit Administration's (FTA) new Public Transportation Emergency Relief Program. An FTA damage assessment in January 2013 estimated the costs of repairing facilities damaged by Hurricane Sandy in New York and New Jersey to be about $5.7 billion. To date, FTA has obligated about $1.5 billion for 15 grants and disbursed about $499 million to reimburse transit agencies for emergency response, recovery, and repair costs. These disbursements are consistent with Congressional Budget Office estimates, and transit projects can take years to complete. Furthermore, FTA plans to use nearly half of its DRAA appropriation for resiliency projects (or projects to protect facilities from future damage), most of which will be carried out through a competitive grant process. FTA was evaluating applications when GAO completed its review.

FTA's new Public Transportation Emergency Relief Program has more flexibility and fewer restrictions in funding projects compared to the Federal Emergency Management Agency's (FEMA) Public Assistance and Hazard Mitigation programs and the Federal Highway Administration's (FHWA) Emergency Relief Program. For example, FEMA's Hazard Mitigation program places limits on the amount of emergency relief funds that can be used for resiliency projects, while FTA's program does not. FTA's program also has more flexibility in how funds can be used for repairs, allowing transit agencies to improve facilities beyond pre-disaster conditions. The use of emergency relief funds for projects that go beyond recovery efforts is not new—activities funded by FHWA's Emergency Relief Program have also expanded beyond repair and reconstruction. The expanding scope of emergency relief assistance illustrates the fiscal exposure the federal government faces and the challenges of establishing long-term sustainable funding for disaster relief and recovery.

Although FTA and FEMA have a memorandum of agreement for assisting transit providers during emergencies, they are limited in their ability to delineate specific roles and responsibilities for future disasters. This limit is because while FEMA receives funding on an ongoing basis, FTA, to date, has only received a supplemental appropriation for Hurricane Sandy and does not know what resources it will have for future disasters. Because FTA and FEMA have the authority to fund many of the same activities by law, transit agencies may experience confusion when seeking assistance under some circumstances. FTA and FEMA have not determined how collaborative efforts, including their communications program and protocol contemplated in the memorandum of agreement, will be monitored, evaluated, and reported, but instead rely on informal communication. As GAO has previously concluded, creating a means to evaluate the results of collaborative efforts can enhance and sustain them, and informal communications between federal agencies do not ensure that collaboration is effective. Establishing more formal monitoring and evaluation of combined efforts could help FTA and FEMA ensure effective collaboration.

\* \* \*

May 28, 2014

The Honorable Tom Latham
Chairman
Subcommittee on Transportation, Housing and Urban Development, and Related Agencies
Committee on Appropriations
House of Representatives

Dear Mr. Chairman:

Public transportation agencies are vulnerable to natural and man-made disasters that can disrupt transit operations and destroy vehicles and facilities. This presents a range of challenges, as transportation infrastructure is a key resource before, during, and after a major disaster or emergency. Before a disaster, public transportation infrastructure and resources can be used to assist with evacuating residents. During a disaster, the loss of transit can worsen the disaster's impact by impeding a community's access to emergency relief services and medical care. After a disaster, public transportation can be used to return people to their homes by restarting normal operations and allowing people to return to their jobs and daily activities.

In October 2012, Hurricane Sandy hit the Mid-Atlantic coast during high tide, bringing with it a storm surge and flooding. The President issued disaster declarations under the Robert T. Stafford Disaster Relief and Emergency Assistance Act (Stafford Act)[1] for the following areas: Connecticut, Delaware, District of Columbia, Maryland, Massachusetts, New Hampshire, New Jersey, New York, Ohio, Pennsylvania, Rhode Island, Virginia, and West Virginia. Parts of New York and New Jersey were the hardest hit, and mobility in the greater New York City metropolitan area was temporarily crippled, including its transit systems, which normally carry more customers than all other systems in the United States combined. In January 2013, the President signed the Disaster Relief Appropriations Act, 2013 (DRAA), which provided approximately $50.5 billion in supplemental appropriations to 61 programs at 19 federal agencies for expenses related to Hurricane Sandy.[2] DRAA provided over $13 billion to the Department of Transportation (DOT), most of it to the Federal Transit Administration's (FTA) new Public Transportation Emergency Relief Program, which had gone into effect 28 days before Hurricane Sandy struck the United States. However, not all of the funds appropriated to FTA under DRAA were available until DOT signed a memorandum of agreement on March 4, 2013, with the Department of Homeland Security (DHS) to coordinate the roles and responsibilities of the two departments in providing assistance for public transportation.[3] The Federal Emergency Management Agency (FEMA), within DHS, is the lead agency responsible for preparing the federal response plans and programs for future disasters, coordinating the federal response when a disaster is declared, and providing grants to assist state and local governments during the response and recovery phases of a disaster. Within DOT, the Federal Highway Administration (FHWA) also has an Emergency Relief Program that provides funds for the repair and reconstruction of roads on the federal-aid highway system that have suffered serious damage as a result of either a natural disaster or a catastrophic failure from any external cause.

Given the amount of funds distributed and the number of agencies involved, you requested that we study emergency relief for transportation facilities and the services being carried out under the DRAA. We reviewed DOT's progress in disbursing DRAA funds to address Hurricane Sandy—with a focus on FTA's new Public Transportation Emergency Relief Program, how it compares to other federal agencies that provide emergency relief funding to surface transportation, and implications for responding to future disasters. Specifically, this report addresses (1) the progress DOT has made allocating, obligating, and disbursing DRAA surface transportation funds; (2) how FTA's new Public Transportation Emergency Relief Program compares to FEMA's and FHWA's emergency relief programs; and (3) the extent to which FTA and FEMA have implemented their memorandum of agreement to coordinate their roles and responsibilities when providing assistance to transit agencies affected by Hurricane Sandy or future disasters.

To address all objectives, we reviewed and analyzed relevant laws and regulations; our previous reports; FTA, FWHA, and FEMA guidance; and interviewed officials from DOT and FEMA. We interviewed officials from seven of the 13 transit agencies that received grants from FTA. We selected the transit agencies that received FTA's four largest funding allocations (all located within New York and New Jersey) and selected three agencies that received smaller funding allocations but were located outside of New York and New Jersey. Our findings from interviews with these selected agencies provide insights and illustrate FTA's emergency transit-relief grant process; however, the results of our review should not be used to make generalizations about all FTA emergency transit relief grants. We also interviewed officials from Amtrak,[4] which received funds from the Federal Railroad Administration (FRA) within DOT.

To determine the progress DOT has made with DRAA surface transportation funds, we obtained information from the DOT surface-transportation agencies—FTA, FHWA, and FRA—on the amount of DRAA funds that have been allocated, obligated, and disbursed from March 2013 to April 2014. We obtained FTA's damage assessment of public transit agencies in New York and New Jersey affected by Hurricane Sandy. We reviewed the Congressional Budget Office's (CBO) 2012 analysis of the DRAA. To assess the reliability of the allocation, obligation, and disbursement data we received from DOT, we reviewed relevant documentation, interviewed knowledgeable officials, and reviewed internal controls related to the handling of the data. We found the data to be sufficiently reliable for our purposes. To determine how FTA's Public Transportation Emergency Relief Program compares to FEMA's and FHWA's emergency relief programs, we reviewed and analyzed relevant statutes and regulations, as well as documents pertaining to FTA, FHWA, and FEMA emergency relief programs to determine similarities and differences between the programs' eligibility rules, requirements, and funding.[5] To determine the extent to which FTA and FEMA have coordinated their roles and responsibilities when providing disaster assistance to transit agencies, we reviewed and analyzed their memorandum of agreement and compared the agencies' efforts to practices that we have found can enhance collaboration among federal agencies.

## BACKGROUND

We conducted this performance audit from April 2013 to May 2014 in accordance with generally accepted government auditing standards. Those standards require that we plan and perform the audit to obtain sufficient, appropriate evidence to provide a reasonable basis for our findings and conclusions based on our audit objectives. We believe that the evidence obtained provides a reasonable basis for our findings and conclusions based on our audit objectives. Appendix I provides a more detailed description of our scope and methodology.

When a disaster overwhelms the ability of state, local, and voluntary agencies to adequately provide essential services on their own, the federal government generally plays a central role in disaster response, providing selected resources where they are needed. The federal government has provided significant funds for transit services following past catastrophic disasters. For example, about $4.7 billion was provided in emergency supplemental appropriations for emergency transit services in response to the September 11, 2001, attacks and $232 million in response to the 2005 Gulf Coast hurricanes.

After Hurricane Sandy, Congress enacted and the President signed into law the DRAA, which provided supplemental appropriations to federal agencies to assist, improve, and streamline Hurricane Sandy recovery efforts, including efforts to address damage to public transportation systems. Figure 1 shows the funding provided by the DRAA by agency, including over $13 billion to DOT.[6]

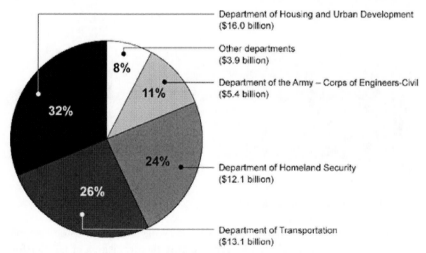

Source: GAO analysis of the Disabled Relief Appropriations Act, 2013.
Note: Percentages do not add to 100 due to rounding.

Figure 1. $50.5 Million in DRAA Funding by Agency (As Enacted on January 29, 2013).

Most of DOT's DRAA funding was made available to assist transit agencies, especially in New York and New Jersey, which experienced substantial damage to their infrastructure and incurred significant costs to restore operational service after the storm. All of these transit systems experienced the temporary suspension of service and most sustained serious, widespread damage, which affected the region's entire transportation network. As alternative modes of travel were sought, the use of the region's roadway network far exceeded capacity. The ripple effects were felt by many residents of the region who were not able to travel. Figure 2 below illustrates some of the damage to regional transportation systems as a result of Hurricane Sandy.

Sandbags at the entrances of Port Authority Trans-Hudson rail transit station in Hoboken, N.J.
Source: Port Authority of New York and New Jersey.

Damage to the Metropolitan Transit Authority Rockaway Line
Source: New York Metropolitan Transportation Authority (MTA).

Flood waters pouring into the Hoboken Station on the Port Authority Trans-Hudson (PATH) System
Source: Port Authority of New York and New Jersey.

Damage to the Morgan Drawbridge on the New Jersey Transit System
Source: New Jersey Transit.

Figure 2. Examples of Damage from Hurricane Sandy.

FEMA is the federal government's primary agency for disaster response and has primary responsibility for administering the provisions of the Stafford Act and for carrying out activities for national preparedness. Specifically, FEMA (1) funds and coordinates eligible prevention, protection, and mitigation activities; (2) provides and coordinates the immediate federal response to save lives and property; (3) funds the reconstruction of disaster-damaged public infrastructure; and (4) provides individual assistance to stricken families. In addition to coordinating disaster response and recovery operations, FEMA's Public Assistance Program provides funding to state and local governments and some nonprofit organizations for recovery efforts after a disaster, including removing debris, implementing emergency protective measures, and repairing or replacing damaged public equipment or facilities. FEMA also provides grants to states and local governments to implement mitigation measures that reduce or permanently eliminate future risk to lives and property from natural hazards under its Hazard Mitigation Grant Program. This program funds projects in accordance with priorities identified in state, tribal, or local hazard mitigation plans and enables mitigation measures to be implemented during the immediate recovery from a disaster.

DOT also has two emergency relief programs to assist with damage to surface transportation infrastructure and facilities after a disaster, both of which received a share of DOT's DRAA funding for Hurricane Sandy.

- FHWA's Emergency Relief Program provides funding for emergency and permanent repairs or reconstruction of roadways on the federal-aid highway system and on federal lands that have suffered serious damage as a result of a natural disaster or catastrophic failure from an external cause. Emergency repairs are completed during and immediately following a disaster to quickly restore essential highway traffic service and protect remaining facilities, for example, establishing emergency detours and providing temporary bridges or ferry service. Permanent repairs are undertaken after emergency repairs have been completed to restore damaged facilities to pre-disaster conditions, for example, restoring pavement surfaces or reconstructing damaged bridges. FHWA only provides funding under its Emergency Relief Program for highways that are either federal-aid highways or on federal lands. FEMA's Public Assistance Program provides funding to repair disaster damage to other roads.

- FTA's Public Transportation Emergency Relief Program was authorized by the Moving Ahead for Progress in the 21st Century Act (MAP-21).[7] MAP-21 provides FTA with the primary responsibility for reimbursing emergency response and recovery costs after an emergency or major disaster affects a public transportation system. The FTA program is a reimbursable grant program and allows FTA to emergency or major disaster affects a public transportation system. The FTA program is a reimbursable grant program and allows FTA to make grants for capital projects to protect, repair, reconstruct, or replace equipment and facilities of a public transportation system as well as for eligible operating costs. Such costs include reestablishing, expanding, or relocating public transportation route service in the event of a natural disaster that affects a wide area or a catastrophic failure from any external cause.

Most of the $13 billion that DRAA made available to DOT for surface transportation relief was appropriated to FTA for the Public Transportation Emergency Relief Program.[8] The DRAA provides this funding for eligible transit operating expenses, capital projects to repair or reconstruct damaged facilities, and projects to protect facilities from future damage (resiliency projects). According to FTA's interim program regulations, resiliency projects are designed and built to address a transit system's future vulnerabilities due to emergencies or major disasters that have occurred and are likely to reoccur in the geographic area in which the public transportation system is located, or projected changes in development patterns, demographics, or extreme weather or other climate patterns.[9] For example, MTA is planning a resiliency project to increase New York City's pumping capacity by converting existing rolling stock into pump trains. The project is intended to shorten the period of time it takes to pump water out of the subway system to prevent major damage from saltwater infiltration into the subway system. The DRAA also provided the DOT Secretary authority to transfer up to $5.4 billion for resiliency efforts to other DOT agencies, such as FHWA and FRA.[10]

In January 2013, FTA, FEMA, and affected transit agencies worked together after Hurricane Sandy to assess the damage in the New York and New Jersey region. The damage assessment estimated that the damage to public transit was about $5.7 billion. About 99 percent of the estimated damage was sustained by four transit agencies, as shown in table 1.

FTA officials said that the damage assessment only covered damage in New York and New Jersey because this was the area with the most extensive damage. Rather than identify total damage in other areas, FTA established a process for potential recipients to identify their damage and to apply for funds. FTA made initial grants to recipients outside of New York and New Jersey, but those grants account for less than 1 percent of all allocations made as of April 30, 2014. For example, FTA awarded a $5,352 grant to the Milford Transit District (MTD) in Connecticut for evacuation services performed during Hurricane Sandy, transportation after the storm, and debris cleanup. Beyond that, FTA has not estimated an amount of repair and recovery outside of New York and New Jersey but has set aside funds for future allocations

(approximately $28 million) as needed if there are eligible response and
recovery expenses from agencies that may not have received pro-rated
allocations.

**Table 1. Estimated Damage to New York and New Jersey Transit
Agencies, As Assessed by FTA, FEMA, and Transit Agencies
(January 31, 2013)**

| Agencies | Restoration/Recovery |
|---|---|
| New York Metropolitan Transportation Authority (MTA) | 3,904 |
| Port Authority of New York/New Jersey | 1,286 |
| New Jersey Transit | 459 |
| New York City DOT | 36 |
| Other New York/New Jersey Agencies | 4 |
| TOTAL | $5,689 |

Source: FTA.

# FTA HAS ALLOCATED OVER HALF OF DOT'S DRAA FUNDS WHILE SETTING UP THE PUBLIC TRANSPORTATION EMERGENCY RELIEF PROGRAM

## Overall DOT Progress

As figure 3 shows, the approximately $13 billion that DRAA appropriated
to DOT for surface transportation relief was divided among several DOT
agencies including FTA, FHWA, and FRA—but the vast majority of it was
appropriated to FTA.

Two events have affected the amount of funds available to the DOT
agencies. First, all DRAA funds were reduced by 5 percent—from
approximately $13 billion to almost $12.4 billion—on March 1, 2013, as a
result of sequestration.[11] Second, the DOT Secretary exercised his transfer
authority under DRAA and approved a transfer in May 2013 of $185 million
from FTA to FRA. This transfer was used to award a grant for Amtrak to
install a concrete casing that preserves the right of way in the New York City
Hudson Yards for the potential alignment of a future trans-Hudson tunnel.

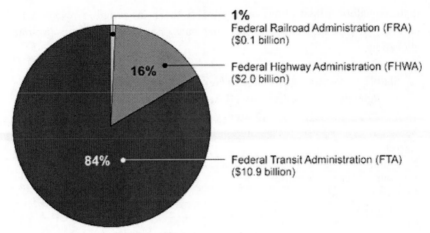

1%
Federal Railroad Administration (FRA)
($0.1 billion)

Federal Highway Administration (FHWA)
($2.0 billion)

Federal Transit Administration (FTA)
($10.9 billion)

Source: GAO analysis of the Disaster Relief Appropriations Act 2013.
Note: Percentages do not add to 100 due to rounding.

Figure 3. DRAA Appropriations for Surface Transportation (As Enacted on January 29, 2013).

This concrete casing would allow access for a future project to install an additional railway tunnel under the Hudson River and increase train capacity for commuter, regional, and long distance intercity services going in and out of New York City (see fig. 4). The Gateway Tunnel project has been planned since 2010, and with this funding, Amtrak is able to preserve a possible right-of-way for the project. DOT officials told us that there are no plans at this time to make any other transfers using this authority.

DOT surface transportation agencies have allocated about $6.3 billion (51 percent), obligated about $2.2 billion (17 percent), and disbursed about $721 million (6 percent) of the roughly $12.4 billion available DRAA funds for transportation relief as of April 30, 2014.[12] The available funds for each agency shown in table 2 reflect the impact of sequestration, and the DOT Secretary's transfer from FTA to FRA.

## FTA Progress

FTA is in the process of allocating and distributing DRAA funds while facing unique challenges setting up its Public Transportation Emergency Relief Program.

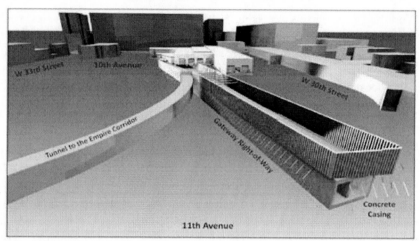

Source: Amtrack.

Figure 4. Depiction of the Amtrak Gateway Tunnel Project between New York and New Jersey.

### Table 2. DOT DRAA Funding Status ($ millions) as of April 30, 2014

| DOT Surface Transportation Administrations | Available funds | Allocated | Obligated | Disbursed |
|---|---|---|---|---|
| Federal Highway Administration | 1,921 | 616 | 473 | 120 |
| Federal Railroad Administration | 297 | a | 215 | 102 |
| Federal Transit Administration | 10,170 | 5,679 | 1,463 | 499 |
| TOTAL | $12,388 | $6,295 | $2,151 | $721 |

Source: DOT.

[a] FRA funds are not allocated to grantees as they are for FHWA and FTA programs; FRA grants are awarded from available funds.

The program was new when Hurricane Sandy struck, and FTA received its first funds for the program through the DRAA just 3 months after the storm. As a result, as of April 2014, FTA was finalizing its program rules at the same time it was distributing billions of dollars of DRAA funds to affected transit agencies. Furthermore, the amount of funds that FTA is distributing through the emergency relief program (over $10 billion) is almost as much as FTA's total budgetary resources were in fiscal year 2012 (approximately $12.1 billion).

FTA's over $10 billion in DRAA funding is more than enough to address the costs of repairing transit facilities damaged by Hurricane Sandy in New

York and New Jersey (see table 1). The January 2013 damage assessment estimated Hurricane Sandy damage in New York and New Jersey to public transit to be about $5.7 billion, but also identified about $10 billion in potential resiliency projects to guard against future disasters. As of April 30, 2014, FTA has allocated almost $5.7 billion of its DRAA funding to transit agencies affected by Hurricane Sandy and obligated a total of about $1.5 billion for 15 grants for emergency response, recovery, repair and reconstruction activities.[13] When we completed our review, transit agency officials we spoke with were generally positive about the FTA Public Transportation Emergency Relief Program and told us that, in their experience, FTA has not caused them any delays in receiving funding. Of the amount allocated, FTA made $1.3 billion available for what it called "locally prioritized" resiliency funding. This funding is primarily intended for resiliency improvements completed in tandem with recovery and rebuilding projects that will improve cost effectiveness and can be implemented quickly.

As of April 30, 2014, FTA has only disbursed $499 million of its DRAA funds, but this does not indicate a lack of progress for several reasons. FTA's progress is in line with expenditure estimates. In December 2012, CBO estimated that only 3 percent of FTA's DRAA funds would be expended in the first year and forecasted that it would take over a decade for FTA to disburse all the funds based on historical patterns.[14] As of January 29, 2014—one year after DRAA was enacted—FTA had disbursed almost 3 percent of its DRAA funds, approaching CBO estimates. In addition, transit projects are long-term investments that typically take years to complete. For example, the MTA Long Island Rail Road's West Side Storage Yard—which undertakes inspections, repairs, maintenance, and cleaning for the railroad's fleet—suffered severe damage due to the tidal surge and resulting intrusion of salt water during Hurricane Sandy. The project to repair it will replace numerous assets in the yard, including switch machines, signal components, third-rail components, switch heaters, and fire alarm systems. According to officials, MTA plans to complete this work in phases and estimates a February 2018 completion. Finally, FTA plans to use about 42 percent of its DRAA appropriation for resiliency projects, most of which will be carried out through a competitive grant selection process, and FTA was evaluating applications when we completed our review.

Specifically, in December 2013, FTA issued a Notice of Funding Availability for approximately $3 billion in funding to be awarded for resiliency projects on a competitive basis.[15] This funding differs from the $1.3 billion that has been obligated for locally prioritized resiliency funding. Any transportation agency[16] within the declared Hurricane Sandy disaster area can apply for these funds,[17] and they can be used to protect either a facility or system that has been repaired or replaced after Hurricane Sandy, or that is at risk of being damaged or destroyed by a future emergency or natural disaster.[18] Among the other criteria, FTA will evaluate and award competitive resiliency funding based on the cost-effectiveness of the project, implementation strategy, extent to which improvements will protect vulnerable existing infrastructure, availability of local financial commitments, and the technical capacity of grantees. According to FTA's notice, in developing FTA guidelines for resiliency projects, it considered recommendations made by the Hurricane Sandy Rebuilding Task Force.[19] The Task Force specifically recommended that infrastructure rebuilt with DRAA funds be designed to increase the resilience of the region.[20]

The DRAA appropriation to FTA provided funding for the DOT Office of Inspector General (OIG) to conduct oversight of FTA's DRAA funds. In the initial report, the OIG stated that FTA's initial response to Hurricane Sandy was noteworthy, but that FTA has yet to fully address challenges in its oversight plans and procedures.[21] The OIG made several recommendations to FTA, including specifying the required time frames for completing risk assessments for all grantees and finalizing program guidance that incorporates lessons learned from emergencies and best practices from emergency relief guidance. According to the OIG's report, FTA has provided appropriate planned actions and timeframes for completion for most of the OIG recommendations.

## FTA's Relief Program Is More Flexible Than FEMA's and FHWA's but Has Not Received Ongoing Funding

Compared to FEMA's Public Assistance and Hazard Mitigation Grant Programs and FHWA's Emergency Relief Program, FTA's new Public Transportation Emergency Relief Program has more flexibility and fewer restrictions in funding emergency relief projects. For example, FEMA's Hazard Mitigation Grant Program places limits on the amount of emergency relief funding that can be allocated toward resiliency projects, whereas FTA's program does not. However, unlike FEMA's and FHWA's programs, FTA's program has not received funding on an ongoing basis, which could limit some transit providers' ability to respond immediately after a disaster.

## FTA's Program Has More Flexibility and Fewer Restrictions

FTA's Public Transportation Emergency Relief Program provides funding for similar types of activities as FEMA's and FHWA's emergency relief programs, such as emergency protective measures, permanent repairs, and resiliency projects, but the legislation authorizing FTA's program placed no limits on the amount that can be awarded for resiliency projects. Based on this flexibility, FTA is awarding about 42 percent of the funding it received for Hurricane Sandy, $4.3 billion, for resiliency projects.

In contrast, FEMA has limits on the percentage of emergency funding that may be used for resiliency projects. FEMA's Hazard Mitigation Grant Program provides funding for resiliency projects (referred to as hazard mitigation projects) but the amount of funding available for this program for a particular disaster declaration is limited. For example, under this program a state may be eligible to receive up to 15 percent of the estimated total of federal assistance for hazard mitigation grant assistance. States that meet higher mitigation planning criteria may qualify for up to 20 percent of assistance.[22] Of the $119.7 billion that FEMA has obligated for disaster assistance over a 10-year period—from 2004 through 2013—FEMA has obligated $4.9 billion (about 4 percent) for its Hazard Mitigation Grant Program activities to prevent or ease the impact of natural disasters.

Besides having greater flexibility in funding resiliency projects, FTA's Public Transportation Emergency Relief Program has fewer restrictions and greater flexibility to fund emergency relief projects compared to FHWA's and FEMA's programs, as discussed below:

*FTA's program funds have more flexibility in how they can be used for repairs.* FTA's Public Transportation Emergency Relief Program allows transit agencies to use response and recovery awards to improve facilities beyond pre-existing conditions by 1) replacing damaged assets with new assets that incorporate current design standards, 2) replacing obsolete equipment, or 3) bringing assets to a state of good repair as part of its recovery effort. By comparison, FEMA's Public Assistance Program will generally provide funding for permanent repairs to restore a facility based on the adopted codes and standards to its pre-disaster design, function, and capacity.[23] FEMA's Public Assistance Program may provide funding to replace the facility to current applicable codes and standards, if the grantee can demonstrate that the estimated repair cost exceeds 50 percent of the estimated replacement cost. FEMA's Public Assistance Program also provides some funding to be used for hazard mitigation measures. This funding, along with FEMA's Hazard Mitigation Program funding, can be used to improve facilities beyond pre-disaster conditions if applicants can demonstrate that the project is cost-effective. Like FTA's program, FHWA's Emergency Relief Program will also provide emergency relief funding to restore or replace a facility or bridge to current geometric and construction standards. However, FHWA limits this funding only to portions of the facility that are damaged and requires applicants to show that the improvement is cost-effective, prevents future recurring damage, or is technically feasible. In addition, FTA has more flexibility in how it can support emergency transit operations. For example, FTA's emergency relief program provides funding for emergency operations such as evacuations; rescue operations; ferry service to replace inoperable rail service or to detour around damaged areas; returning evacuees to their home after Hurricane Sandy; and for the net project costs related to reestablishing, expanding, or relocating public transportation service before, during or after Hurricane Sandy. By comparison, under FEMA's Public Assistance Program, financial assistance for transit and transportation operations are limited to those operations that are necessary to save lives and protect public health, such as evacuation or transportation of evacuees to emergency shelter. According to FEMA officials, FEMA does not have the authority to reimburse state or local transit agencies for expenses associated with emergency transit operations.

*FTA emergency relief funds have no restrictions on funding projects included in statewide transportation improvement programs.* FTA emergency relief funds can be used to fund projects that are included in statewide transportation improvement programs. In comparison, under MAP-21, FHWA emergency relief funds may not be used to repair or reconstruct a bridge if the construction phase of a replacement structure is already included in the approved statewide transportation improvement program at the time of an eligible event. Similarly, according to FEMA's Pubic Assistance Program guidance, funding may not be used to replace a facility if the facility is already scheduled to be replaced using federal funds, and work is scheduled to begin within 12 months of the time the disaster struck. According to FTA officials, funding for projects in statewide transportation improvement programs are not limited because FTA does not believe such plans constitute a firm commitment of funding.

**Table 3. Federal and Non-Federal Cost-Sharing Arrangements for FTA's,**
**FEMA's, and FHWA's Emergency Relief Programs**

| Agency | Program | Federal share | Non-federal share |
|--------|---------|---------------|-------------------|
| FTA | Public Transportation Emergency Relief Program | Up to 80 percent of the project cost.[a] | Not less than 20 percent of the project cost. |
| FEMA | Public Assistance Program | Not less than 75 percent of the eligible project cost.[b] | Not more than 25 percent of the projectcost. |
| | Hazard Mitigation Program | Up to 75 percent of the eligible activity costs. | Not less than 25 percent of eligible activity costs. |
| FHWA | Emergency Relief Program | Up to 100 percent for emergency repairs completed within 180 days after a disaster.[c] For permanent repair costs and emergency repair costs incurred after the first 180 days, the federal share is based on the type of federal-aid highway being repaired.d | Varies depending on the type of federalaid highway. |

Source: GAO analysis of FTA, FEMA, and FHWA information.

[a] The DOT Secretary is authorized to adjust cost shares for the program and to waive in whole or in part the non-federal share requirement.

[b] Sections 403, 406, 407, and 502 of the Stafford Act provide that the Federal share of assistance shall be not less than 75 percent of the cost of the eligible work. FEMA regulations at section 206.47 of title 44, C.F.R., allow FEMA to recommend an increased cost-share. For example, in response to Hurricane Sandy, for the state of New York, the President authorized federal funds for all categories of the Public Assistance Program at 90 percent of total eligible costs, except assistance previously designated at 100 percent Federal share. In addition, FEMA recommends raising the usual 75 percent federal share for the Public Assistance Program to 90 percent when federal obligations, excluding FEMA administrative costs, meet a qualifying threshold.

[c] Emergency repairs completed within 180 days after a disaster to restore essential travel, minimize the extent of damage, or protect the remaining facilities are eligible for a 100 percent federal share.

[d] For example, for interstate highways, the federal share is 90 percent. For federal-aid facilities that meet the definition of a federal land access transportation facility, the federal share is 100 percent and for all other highways, the federal share is 80 percent. In addition, MAP-21 provided authority for the Secretary of Transportation to extend the 180-day period for 100 percent federal share of emergency repair work if there is a delay in the state's ability to access the site.

However, projects for which funds were obligated in an FTA grant prior to the declared emergency or disaster are not eligible to receive FTA emergency relief funds.[24]

*FTA's cost-sharing arrangements and rules for non-federal sharing commitments are less restrictive.* As shown in table 3, cost-sharing arrangements vary among FTA's, FEMA's, and FHWA's emergency relief programs. Under FTA's program, for example, the federal share for capital and operating costs is generally up to 80 percent, and the nonfederal share is generally not less than 20 percent of the project cost. However, the DOT Secretary is authorized to waive in whole or in part FTA's non-federal share. Pursuant to the Stafford Act, the cost-sharing arrangements for FEMA's Public Assistance Program can also be adjusted, but only by the President at a governor's request.

In addition, FTA's program permits recipients to waive local matching requirements by applying toll credits toward the non-federal match. Recipients of FHWA's Emergency Relief Program funds are specifically prohibited from using toll credits to reduce or eliminate the non-federal share.[25] States and localities that receive federal formula funds for highway or transit projects may apply "toll credits" to reduce or eliminate the funding they are required to provide to match federal funds for projects. These toll credits are earned when the state, a toll authority, or a private entity funds a capital transportation investment with toll revenues earned from existing toll facilities. FEMA's Public Assistance and Hazard Mitigation Programs also do not allow for applicants to apply toll credits toward the local match but have other ways of meeting the non-federal share amount, for example, through in-kind contributions.[26]

*FTA's program does not require a presidential declaration of disaster to release emergency relief funds.* Under both FTA's and FHWA's programs, for a natural disaster or other event to be eligible for emergency relief funding, either the governor of a state has to declare an emergency and the Secretary of Transportation has to concur, or the President has to declare a major disaster under section 401 of the Stafford Act. However, a Presidential Declaration of a Major Disaster or Emergency is required for funding to be available for FEMA's Public Assistance Program. Likewise, FEMA's Hazard Mitigation Program requires a presidential declaration of a major disaster for funding to be available for that program.

*FTA's program has flexibility to provide funds directly to the grantee.* Under FEMA's and FHWA's programs, funding is distributed to the states. FEMA provides funding under its Public Assistance Program to eligible applicants through state and tribal government grantees. In our prior work, we found instances where funding from state grantees to transit agencies was delayed.[27] FHWA's Emergency Relief Program similarly provides funding to states, Puerto Rico, the District of Columbia, and territories. The program is administered through the state DOTs in close coordination with FHWA's division offices in each state. In contrast, FTA funding can be provided directly to transit agencies. Officials from the grantee agencies we spoke to told us that working with FTA is easier than working with FEMA, in part because of their ongoing grantee relationship with FTA and because FTA's personnel are transit specialists and its processes are better suited for complicated transit projects.

## Recent Changes Have Expanded the Scope of Activities FHWA and FEMA May Fund

Even though FTA has more flexibility, particularly in the amount of funding it can allocate to resiliency projects, several recent changes to FHWA and FEMA program requirements have further expanded the scope of activities eligible for funding under these programs.

- MAP-21 expanded FHWA's scope of activities to allow its emergency relief funds to be used to expand the capacity of a structure—such as bridges, highways, or roads—being repaired or replaced to accommodate the volume of traffic that the structure will carry over its design life.[28] Prior to MAP-21, FHWA's Emergency Relief Program could only be used to expand the capacity of bridges to accommodate future traffic.
- The Sandy Recovery Improvement Act of 2013 [29] revised the Stafford Act, establishing a new set of alternative procedures for FEMA's Public Assistance Program, allowing applicants to receive funding based on fixed estimates, rather than being reimbursed for actual costs. Under these new procedures, applicants can use grant funding that exceeds actual costs toward mitigation activities.

Use of emergency relief funds for projects that go beyond recovery efforts is not new. In our 2007 report on FHWA's Emergency Relief Program, we found that FHWA's use of Emergency Relief Program funds was not always limited to rebuilding facilities back to original conditions—the original intent of the program—and were used for projects that had grown in size and scope in response to public and community concerns.[30] For example, emergency relief funds were used to fund the reconstruction of the U.S. Highway 90 Biloxi Bay Bridge in Mississippi, a four-lane drawbridge between the cities of Biloxi and Ocean Springs, Mississippi. According to the Mississippi DOT officials, DOT initially proposed replacing the drawbridge with one that would provide an 85-foot clearance above Biloxi Bay. During a public comment period on the proposed bridge design, a local shipbuilder expressed concern that the height was not sufficient to allow for future ships to pass under the bridge. Mississippi DOT revised its proposed bridge design to provide a 95-foot clearance, which increased the cost of the bridge from an estimated $275 million to $339 million. We have also found that Congress has, on occasion, expanded FHWA's and FEMA's emergency relief eligibility criteria, an expansion that has resulted in projects receiving funding beyond what FHWA's and FEMA's emergency relief programs would otherwise have funded.[31] For example, in 2003, following the September 11, 2001, terrorist attack, Congress appropriated supplemental funding expanding FEMA's authority to allow it to fund recovery efforts and rebuild infrastructure beyond pre-disaster conditions to substantially improve commuter mobility.

While we have previously raised concerns about the expanding scope of activities eligible for emergency relief funding, we have also noted that building resiliency into infrastructure planning is important. [32] Enhancing the resilience of physical infrastructure, such as roads and bridges, vulnerable to extreme weather conditions can help reduce future economic losses and result in more efficient infrastructure planning. Federally funded road and bridge projects are typically expensive longterm investments. We have previously concluded that as the nation makes these investments, it faces the choice of paying more now, or potentially paying a much larger premium later to repair, modify, or replace infrastructure ill suited for future conditions.[33]

## FTA's Public Transportation Emergency Relief Program Does Not Currently Receive Funding on an Ongoing Basis

FEMA and FHWA have funds available to provide recovery assistance when a disaster or emergency occurs:

- Funding for FEMA's Public Assistance and Hazard Mitigation Programs is available from the Disaster Relief Fund (DRF) after the President declares a disaster under the Stafford Act.34 The DRF receives emergency-designated funding through both the regular appropriations process and through supplemental appropriations. The amount requested each year for the DRF in the President's Budget Request is based on the use of the fund (amount obligated from the fund) in prior years.35 Once funds are appropriated to the DRF, they are available until expended, which means they carry forward from one year to another.

- Budget authority for FHWA's Emergency Relief Program is provided through contract authority, which authorizes FHWA to make commitments in advance of an appropriation. 36 FHWA is authorized to obligate up to $100 million each fiscal year for the program. Any unobligated balance remains available until expended.[37] In recent years, annual demands on FHWA's Emergency Relief Program have exceeded the $100 million annual authorization. For example, on average, the program's needed allocations for ordinary events—disaster events requiring under $100 million in federal funding—are 2.7 times the annual authorization, or $271 million. As a result, from 2005 to 2011, FHWA received about $7 billion in additional funding from general revenues through supplemental appropriations.

To date, Congress has not provided an annual appropriation for FTA's Public Transportation Emergency Relief Program, and FTA must rely on Congress to appropriate funds for a specific event. FTA's program has only received funds that Congress made available exclusively for Hurricane Sandy through the DRAA. Since it takes time for appropriations to be enacted, FTA is unable to release funding immediately after a disaster to transit providers which, in turn, could limit the ability of transit agencies that do not have resources to respond immediately after a disaster. However, annual budgeting for FTA's emergency relief program through regular appropriations would involve trade-offs with other funding priorities in a challenging budget environment. Events requiring the use of FEMA and FHWA emergency funds generally occur every year; however, transit disasters requiring FTA emergency relief funding may occur with less frequency. Ultimately, deciding how to allocate funding among competing demands is a policy decision for the Congress.

We discussed transit-funding challenges in our 2008 report, which highlighted the impact of challenges on the timeliness and effectiveness of FEMA's and FTA's assistance to transit agencies following the 2005 Gulf Coast hurricanes.[38] We found that neither FEMA nor FTA had mechanisms in place to provide transit funding immediately after the disasters. Transit officials from the New Orleans Regional Transit Authority (NORTA) told us that a lack of financial resources immediately after Hurricane Katrina delayed their disaster response efforts. Based on this work, we presented a range of possible options for Congress to consider for providing immediate financial assistance to transit agencies in response to a disaster, including that Congress create an emergency relief program in FTA for transit assistance modeled after FHWA's program with a "quick release mechanism"—a mechanism used to approve and release emergency funds within 1-2 days to begin the immediate flow of funds.[39] FHWA's program provides for a quick release of funding for larger disasters, wherein extensive damage is readily evident and state and federal level agencies need funds to flow quickly to the state. However, as we previously stated, to date, FTA has not received funding. If FTA's emergency relief program continues to receive only supplemental appropriations, FTA will not be able to quickly release funding for transit operations during and immediately after a disaster occurs.[40]

## Long-standing Challenges of Identifying Long-term Sustainable Funding for Emergency Relief Efforts Remain

The expanding scope of emergency relief assistance and FTA's funding issues illustrate the long-standing challenges of establishing long-term sustainable funding for disaster relief and recovery.

In 2013, we concluded that the federal government does not fully budget for emergency response and recovery costs and runs the risk of facing a large fiscal exposure at any time.[41] Over recent decades, the scope of emergency relief assistance has expanded, with disaster declarations increasing to a record of 98 in fiscal year 2011, compared with 65 in 2004, resulting in increased federal disaster costs. Over that period, FEMA obligated over $80 billion in federal assistance for disasters.[42] The federal government's fiscal exposure will only increase with the financial risks posed by extreme weather events. For this and other reasons, limiting the federal government's fiscal exposure by better managing climate change risks was added to GAO's High-Risk List.

- In our 2007 review of the FHWA Emergency Relief Program, we cited concerns about the use of emergency relief funds on an expanding scope of activities, noting that this gradual expansion of eligibility criteria was exacerbating the problem of longer-term sustainability.[43] We found that monies authorized from the Highway Trust Fund were not sufficient to cover the costs of ordinary events states experienced and that since 1990, the program had relied on supplemental appropriations to make up for the funding shortfall. We recommended that to put the Emergency Relief Program on a sound financial footing, additional alternatives to address the fiscal imbalance needed to be considered and that Congress could consider tightening the eligibility criteria for Emergency Relief funding, either through amending the purpose of the Emergency Relief Program, or by directing FHWA to revise its program regulations. We also recommended that Congress consider the expected future demands of the program and reexamine the appropriate level and sources of funding to address disasters—including whether to increase the $100-million annual authorized funding and whether the Highway Trust Fund, general revenues, or some combination would allow the program to accomplish its purpose in a fiscally sustainable matter.

- In another 2008 report, we reviewed supplemental emergency appropriations from fiscal years 1997–2006 and stated that to the extent possible, funds should be provided through the regular appropriations process to ensure that trade-offs are made among competing priorities, especially in an environment of increasingly constrained resources. [44]

Others have also commented on the process of funding emergency relief efforts in a fiscally sustainable manner. In its 2010 Report, the National Commission on Fiscal Responsibility and Reform[45] recommended that Congress explicitly set aside funds for disaster relief to better prepare for disasters. In a 2003 report, the Congressional Research Service (CRS) cited various challenges and benefits to having an emergency relief fund.[46] For example, according to CRS, maintaining emergency funds at a level that more accurately reflects emergency needs instead of relying on supplemental funding would foster fiscal responsibility and help ensure disaster response funding is budgeted with existing funds. However, CRS noted that, because disasters cannot always be anticipated, emergency supplemental appropriations can facilitate funding recovery efforts for disasters, the timing and severity of which are unpredictable.

# FTA AND FEMA HAVE LIMITED ABILITY TO ASSIGN RESPONSIBILITIES IN THEIR MEMORANDUM OF AGREEMENT BUT COULD DO MORE TO ENSURE EFFECTIVE COLLABORATION

## FTA's and FEMA's Ability to Clarify Specific Responsibilities for Future Disasters Is Limited

On March 4, 2013, FTA and FEMA signed a memorandum of agreement, as required by MAP-21, to coordinate their roles and responsibilities when providing assistance for public transportation in areas in which the President has declared a major disaster or emergency. We have found that by working together to define roles and responsibilities in collaborative efforts, federal agencies can clarify understanding about who will do what, organize their joint and individual efforts, and facilitate decision making.[47] However, in this memorandum of agreement, FTA and FEMA have limited ability to clarify who will do what related to their respective responsibilities when providing emergency transportation relief in future disasters. This is because, as we stated previously, FTA lacks the funding to assume costs for future disasters unless and until Congress provides an appropriation, either on an ongoing basis or for a specific disaster. Lacking information on the resources it will have, FTA is limited in pre-determining what assistance it could provide during future disasters. Conversely, because FHWA receives funding on an ongoing basis, FHWA and FEMA can delineate specific roles and responsibilities during emergencies that affect highways. FHWA provides funds to repair and replace disaster-damaged roads that are on the federal-aid highway system, and FEMA provides funds for roads that are not part of the system. However, FTA and FEMA are limited to more general descriptions of how they will cooperate—such as the principles and general areas of cooperation described in the memorandum of agreement. FEMA officials told us that after FTA finalizes all of its program rules, they may be able to make some small clarifications to their roles and responsibilities, but because of the uncertainty of FTA funding, they will not be able to draw clear distinctions in responsibilities, as they have been able to do with FHWA.

As a result, FTA and FEMA will have to determine their specific roles and responsibilities on a per-incident basis. Funds provided for the FTA Public Transportation Emergency Relief Program do not affect the ability of any other agency to provide any other funds authorized by law. Thus, FEMA and FTA can fund many of the same activities.[48] The memorandum of agreement states that if FTA receives funds, it will be the "primary" payor of expenses incurred by public transportation agencies as a result of emergency or major disaster. For Hurricane Sandy, FTA and FEMA agreed that FTA would assume this responsibility for affected transit agencies, because it received an appropriation from the DRAA large enough to cover the damage without FEMA funding. However, outside of Hurricane Sandy, FTA has been unable to assist transit agencies at all. For example, a transit agency in Massachusetts that had received assistance after Hurricane Sandy from FTA also sustained damage related to Winter Storm Nemo but went to FEMA for assistance instead.[49]

Although FTA had the authority to respond, and the transit agency official said that he preferred to go to FTA, FTA had no funding for any event outside of Hurricane Sandy and could not assist. In the future, agencies may continue to receive transit funding from FTA in one disaster and from FEMA in another. However, if a significant transit disaster occurs in the future and FTA funds are not enough to address the damage, transit agencies could go to FTA to fund some of their repairs and to FEMA to fund others, which could increase confusion and the chance that similar activities could be funded by both agencies inadvertently.

Furthermore, if FTA ultimately does receive supplemental funding after a specific emergency or disaster, transit agencies that receive assistance may have to change their application for emergency funds mid-stream from FEMA to FTA. In the immediate aftermath of Hurricane Sandy, FTA and FEMA officials were uncertain as to which agency would ultimately fund recovery efforts for transit. Transit agency officials affected by the storm said that at first, they were using FEMA worksheets to document their expenses. However, 3 months after the storm—after FTA received an appropriation under DRAA and became the primary payor of expenses—transit agencies had to re-do their paperwork. For example, one transit agency official told us that he put together a lot of documentation after Hurricane Sandy to receive funds from FEMA, documentation that was not necessary when the process changed to FTA. Another transit agency official told us that the requirements for FEMA's and FTA's programs are different and as a result, the agency had to make a change from ensuring FEMA's requirements were met in the application process to ensuring that FTA's requirements were met. Since FEMA's and FTA's programs have different statutory requirements, the agencies are limited in creating standardized procedures that would meet the requirements of both programs. Thus, transit agencies may be uncertain which program requirements they must meet until recovery efforts are well under way, as was the case with Hurricane Sandy.

## FTA and FEMA Could Take Additional Steps to Help Ensure Effective Collaboration

Because FTA and FEMA face challenges assuming definitive and stable roles and responsibilities, it is especially important that they collaborate effectively. Among the practices that we have identified that can enhance and sustain the collaborative efforts of federal agencies is creating a means to monitor, evaluate, and report the results of collaborative efforts to better identify areas for improvement. Reporting on these activities can help key decision makers within the agencies, as well as clients and stakeholders, to obtain feedback for improving both policy and operation effectiveness.[50] We have identified implementation approaches among agencies that successfully monitored progress including developing performance measures and tying them to shared outcomes, identifying and sharing relevant agency performance data, developing methods to report on the group's progress that are open and transparent, and incorporating interagency group activities into individual performance expectations.[51]

FTA and FEMA have not implemented a method to monitor or evaluate their collaborative efforts or report on how well they are working. Instead, FTA and FEMA officials have noted that they meet regularly and notify each other of all grant awards to prevent duplication of DRAA funding. However, we have reported in the past that routine interagency meetings can be dutifully attended without communicating any substantive information. Thus, simply meeting does not guarantee that collaboration is effective.[52] Further, while FTA and FEMA officials state that they are collaborating now on the distribution of DRAA funds, it is unclear how the agencies might work together during future disasters. For example, the memorandum of agreement that MAP-21 required stated that "FTA and FEMA will work together to develop a communications protocol and implement an effective communications program to ensure all interested parties are aware of their respective responsibilities for emergency preparedness, response, and recovery related to public transportation matters." FTA and FEMA officials stated that their informal meetings to discuss DRAA funding serve as the communications protocol indentified in the memorandum of agreement. FTA officials told us that they do not have a communications protocol for anything beyond DRAA funding, because they do not have funding outside of DRAA. However, the requirement to develop the memorandum of agreement to improve coordination was intended to frame the relationship of FTA and FEMA going forward to address transportation emergency activities, not just one disaster. Further, without a means to monitor, evaluate, and report the results of collaborative efforts—including FTA's and FEMA's communication program and protocols— it is unclear how FTA and FEMA officials would know if their collaborative methods were effective. In a future disaster, informal meetings between FTA and FEMA may not be sufficient to ensure that effective collaboration is taking place, particularly if both agencies are funding public transportation activities.

## CONCLUSION

The scope of activities eligible for transportation emergency relief has expanded over time to include funding resiliency efforts that repair and restore facilities beyond pre-disaster conditions. FTA's new Public Transportation Emergency Relief Program was designed to be more flexible when funding resiliency compared to existing disaster-relief programs within FHWA and FEMA, although the scope of activities eligible for funding under those programs have expanded as well. Furthermore, the DRAA provided, through FTA, a significant investment in resiliency and protection against future disasters and funding well beyond (almost twice as much as) the repair and recovery needs of New York and New Jersey, as well as significant flexibility on how to provide those funds to areas affected by Hurricane Sandy. Going forward, as FTA begins awarding funding for resiliency projects through DRAA, the scope of these projects may exceed costs of projects that have previously been funded through historically established emergency relief programs in FHWA and FEMA. Resiliency funding can represent an efficient use of funds that avoids the need for repair and recovery from future disasters. We have reported on the need to build resiliency into infrastructure decision making and the challenges of doing so. However, expanding the scope of activities eligible for transportation emergency relief can pose challenges to providing long-term sustainable funding for disasters. As we have previously reported, the amount of emergency relief funding available is limited in an austere budget environment and may not be sustainable if federal disaster costs continue to increase. As the scope of eligible activities for emergency relief funding continues to expand, additional demands are placed on emergency relief funding further exacerbating the problem of longer-term sustainability. Determining the appropriate limits on emergency relief eligibility criteria will involve tradeoffs and require weighing competing demands in the current budget environment. We have made recommendations in the past on this matter and are therefore not making new recommendations in this report.

Looking beyond Hurricane Sandy relief, FTA's Public Transportation Emergency Relief Program is inherently limited by its inability to fund any activities—recovery or resiliency—without specific congressional action. This limitation has two notable effects. First, FTA cannot immediately respond to disasters involving transit when they occur, such as providing a "quick release" of funds to transit agencies, as was the case with Hurricane Katrina. Second, FTA and FEMA are limited in their ability to clearly delineate the responsibilities and costs each agency will assume during future disasters. As a result, FTA's and FEMA's programs will continue to have the authority and potential to fund the same transit activities, fostering confusion and difficulties for applicants seeking federal assistance in the days after a disaster. This confusion could be exacerbated if a future transit disaster occurred and FTA funding was not sufficient to address recovery needs without FEMA funds and transit agencies had to go to both agencies for the same disaster. Over time, the decision to provide funding authority to any particular agency has proved difficult and the broader challenges of funding disasters involves tradeoffs and requires weighing competing demands. In the meantime, FTA and FEMA can take steps to ensure that within the scope of activities they can control, their collaborative efforts are working. Although the agencies have a memorandum of agreement, FTA and FEMA have not developed any means to monitor, evaluate or report on their collaboration. Furthermore, should FTA receive regular, ongoing funding sometime in the future, then it and FEMA could take action to more clearly delineate roles and responsibilities and identify the costs each agency should assume.

## RECOMMENDATION FOR EXECUTIVE ACTION

We recommend that the Secretary of Transportation and the Secretary of Homeland Security direct the Administrators of FTA and FEMA to establish specific guidelines to monitor, evaluate, and report the results of collaborative efforts—including their communications program and protocol— for Hurricane Sandy as well as future disasters.

## AGENCY COMMENTS

We provided a draft of this report to DOT and DHS for its review and comment. DHS agreed with our recommendation and DOT took no position. DHS and DOT each provided technical comments, which we incorporated as appropriate.

Sincerely yours,
David Wise
Director, Physical Infrastructure Issues

## APPENDIX I: OBJECTIVES, SCOPE, AND METHODOLOGY

This report examines 1) the progress the Department of Transportation (DOT) has made allocating, obligating, and disbursing the Disaster Relief Appropriations Act , 2013 (DRAA) surface transportation funds; 2) how the Federal Transit Administration's (FTA) new emergency relief program compares to the Federal Emergency Management Agency's (FEMA) and Federal Highway Administration's (FHWA) emergency relief programs; and 3) the extent to which FTA and FEMA have implemented their memorandum of agreement to coordinate their roles and responsibilities when providing assistance to transit agencies affected by Hurricane Sandy or future disasters.

To address all three objectives, we reviewed and analyzed relevant laws and regulations and our previous reports. We interviewed headquarters officials responsible for emergency relief programs and budgeting at FEMA, FTA, FHWA, and the Federal Railroad Administration (FRA). We also interviewed FTA regional officials responsible for emergency transit relief in New York and New Jersey, spoke with New York state officials and obtained background on the effects of Hurricane Sandy, and observed residual damage to transit facilities in New York and New Jersey. We interviewed officials from seven of the 13 local transit agencies that received grants from FTA.[1] We selected the transit agencies that received FTA's four largest funding allocations (all located within New York and New Jersey), as well as three agencies that received smaller funding allocations outside of New York and New Jersey. While our observations of these agencies provide key insights and illustrate FTA's emergency transit relief grant process, the results of our review should not be used to make generalizations about all FTA emergency transit relief grants. We also interviewed Amtrak—the sole grantee that received emergency relief grants from FRA (funds that had been transferred from FTA).[2] We did not interview FHWA grantees, as they did not receive any transferred FTA funds.

To determine the progress DOT has made allocating, obligating, and disbursing DRAA surface transportation funds from March 2013 to April 2014, we obtained and analyzed the financial information from DOT's surface transportation agencies (FTA, FHWA, and FRA) on Hurricane Sandy relief allocations, obligations, and disbursements. We also reviewed the FTA's Hurricane Sandy damage assessment of public transit agencies and the 2012 Congressional Budget Office analysis of the DRAA as well as FTA's announcements of Hurricane Sandy disaster relief availability of funds, interim rules, and allocations of funds published in the Federal Register. To access the reliability of the data we reviewed relevant documentation, interviewed knowledgeable officials, and reviewed internal controls. We found the data to be sufficiently reliable for our purposes.

To determine how FTA's new emergency relief program compares to FEMA's and FHWA's emergency relief programs, we interviewed headquarters officials responsible for emergency relief programs at FTA, FHWA, and FEMA.[3] In addition, we reviewed and analyzed applicable authorizing legislation for emergency relief programs for FEMA,[4] FTA,[5] and FHWA.[6] We also reviewed and analyzed emergency relief program regulations, procedures, guidance, and other agency documents on emergency relief at FEMA, FTA, and FHWA to determine similarities and differences between the programs' eligibility rules and requirements (see table 4). Finally, we reviewed independent reports on budgeting for emergency relief,[7] and our past reports on emergency relief efforts.[8]

## Table 4. Agency Guidance Reviewed

| Source | Guidance reviewed |
|---|---|
| Department of Homeland Security, FEMA | |
| | *FEMA 322 Public Assistance Guide, June 2007* |
| | *FEMA 323 Applicant Handbook, March 2010* |
| | *FEMA 321 Public Assistance Policy Digest, January 2008* |
| | *FY 2013 508 Hazard Mitigation Assistance Guidance Unified Guidance,* (July 12, 2013) |
| | *Final Addendum to the Hazard Mitigation Assistance Unified Guidance,* (July 12, 2013) |

**Table 4. (Continued)**

| Source | Guidance reviewed |
|--------|-------------------|
| Department of Transportation, FTA | |
| | Notice of Availability of FTA Emergency Relief Funds in Response to Hurricane Sandy, 78Federal Register 8691 (Feb. 6, 2013). |
| | Notice of Allocation of Public Transportation Emergency Relief Funds in Response to Hurricane Sandy, 78 Fed. Reg. 19357 (March 29, 2013). |
| | Issuance of Interim Final Rule, FTA Emergency Relief Program, 78 Federal Register 19136 (March 29, 2013). |
| | Notice of Second Allocation of Public Transportation Emergency Relief Funds in Response to Hurricane Sandy: Response, Recovery and Resiliency, 78 Federal Register 32296 (May 29, 2013). |
| | Transit Emergency Relief Program, Disaster Relief Appropriations Act of 2013, Grant Making and Grant Management Toolkit, (Apr. 12, 2013). |
| | Notice of Funding Availability for Resilience Projects in Response to Hurricane Sandy, 78 Fed. Reg. 78486 (Dec. 26, 2013). |
| Department of Transportation, FHWA | |
| | *Emergency Relief Manual (Federal-Aid Highways),*(May 31, 2013). |
| | *A Guide to the Federal-Aid Highway Emergency Relief Program,*(Nov. 5, 2012). |

Source: GAO.

To determine the extent to which FTA and FEMA have implemented their memorandum of agreement to coordinate their roles and responsibilities when providing assistance to transit agencies affected by Hurricane Sandy or future disasters, we reviewed and analyzed the mandated memorandum of agreement between FTA and FEMA dated March 4, 2013 and compared the agencies' efforts to practices that we have found can enhance collaboration among federal agencies.[9] We evaluated the extent to which the memorandum of agreement defined roles and responsibilities, assigned costs, specified a system for monitoring and evaluating collaborative efforts, and established communication protocols. We developed a list of evaluation questions based upon the requirements of FTA's Public Transportation Emergency Relief Program authorization in MAP-21 and funding requirements in DRAA. Three GAO team members independently analyzed the memorandum of agreement. The analyses were then consolidated and agreed to by the team members and reviewed by the GAO team's Assistant Director. We also reviewed the DOT OIG report on FTA's oversight of emergency relief funds for coordination between FTA and FEMA for transit relief grants.[10]

We conducted this performance audit from April 2013 to May 2014 in accordance with generally accepted government auditing standards. Those standards require that we plan and perform the audit to obtain sufficient, appropriate evidence to provide a reasonable basis for our findings and conclusions based on our audit objectives. We believe that the evidence obtained provides a reasonable basis for our findings and conclusions based on our audit objectives.

## End Notes

[1] The Robert T. Stafford Disaster Relief and Emergency Assistance Act, as amended April 2013, establishes the authority under which states request a presidential disaster declaration. The act also established the programs and process through which the federal government provides disaster assistance to state and local governments, tribes, and certain nonprofit organizations and individuals. 42 U.S.C. §§ 5121-5207.

[2] Pub. L. No. 113-2 div. A, 127 Stat. 4 (Jan. 29, 2013).

[3] The Moving Ahead for Progress in the 21st Century Act (MAP-21) requires that the Secretaries of the Departments of Homeland Security and Transportation enter a memorandum of agreement to improve coordination between the two departments in providing assistance for public transportation and expedite the provision of federal assistance relating to a major disaster or emergency declared by the President under the Stafford Act. Pub. L. No. 112-141, § 20017(b), 126 Stat. 405, 705 (July 6, 2012). FTA and the Federal Emergency Management Agency (FEMA) entered into the memorandum of agreement on behalf of DOT and DHS respectively.

[4] The National Railroad Passenger Corporation (Amtrak).

[5] During the review the team held coordination meetings with the DOT OIG. We learned they are conducting an extensive multi-phase review of how FTA's Public Transportation Emergency Relief program is being set up and FTA's efforts to ensure that DRAA funds are distributed appropriately. Thus, the team made a decision to focus our review on how the program is structured compared to previously established emergency relief programs in FEMA and FHWA instead of conducting an in-depth evaluation of FTA's Public Transportation Emergency Relief Program at this time.

[6] According to CBO, this law increased nondefense discretionary appropriations for fiscal year 2013 by more than $50 billion and defense discretionary appropriations by over $100 million.

[7] Pub. L. No. 112-141, § 20017(a), 126 Stat 405, 703, codified at 49 U.S.C. § 5324.

[8] FTA's DRAA appropriation has "no-year authority." No-year authority or no-year funding refers to appropriations that do not restrict the time by which funds must be obligated. The DRAA requires that funds for surface transportation grants be expended by grantees within 24 months following the obligation of funds for the grant, unless the Director of the Office of Management and Budget (OMB) waives the requirement and notifies the congressional

Committees on Appropriations. On July 9, 2013, OMB waived this requirement for FTA, FRA, and FHWA.

[9] 49 C.F.R. § 602.5.

[10] These projects must be authorized under titles 23 or 49 of the United States Code, which primarily pertain to highways and bridges, and rail and transit, respectively.

[11] The absence of legislation to reduce the federal budget deficit by at least $1.2 trillion by fiscal year 2021 triggered the sequestration process in section 251A of the Balanced Budget and Emergency Deficit Control Act of 1985 as amended. On March 1, 2013, the President ordered a sequestration of $85.3 billion in discretionary appropriations and direct spending for fiscal year 2013. OMB calculated that this would amount to a 5 percent reduction in nonexempt nondefense discretionary funding for the fiscal year.

[12] For purposes of this report, "allocated" reflects the amount of available funds that have been assigned by DOT to a grantee from which grants may be awarded. "Obligated" reflects the amount of funds legally committed by DOT to a grantee for awarded grants. "Disbursed" reflects the amount of payments that have been made to a grantee.

[13] In March 2013, FTA allocated $2 billion (less almost $21 million to fund expenses for FTA administration and oversight by the DOT OIG) to affected recipients for eligible emergency response and recovery costs including (1) $576.6 million to reimburse affected transit agencies for emergency response and recovery costs incurred or budgeted to date and (2) $1.4 billion primarily to the four agencies most severely impacted (see table 1) for repair and reconstruction projects. These reimbursements are proportional to each agency's estimated overall recovery costs. The $1.4 billion includes the FTA set-aside of approximately $28 million for other affected agencies that may have additional response and recovery expenses not reimbursed to date. In May 2013, FTA allocated an additional $3.7 billion to the four agencies most severely affected, based on a percentage of the anticipated full cost of recovery and rebuilding.

[14] Congressional Budget Office, Estimate of the Disaster Relief Appropriations Act, 2013, as Posted on the website of the Senate Committee on Appropriations on December 12, 2012 (Washington, D.C.: Dec. 12, 2012).

[15] 78 Fed. Reg. 78486 (Dec.26, 2013).

[16] These funds are available for states, local governmental authorities, tribal governments, and other FTA recipients within the declared Hurricane Sandy disaster area. Entities that provide public transportation service and are not current recipients of FTA funding are only eligible to receive emergency relief funding as a subrecipient of an FTA recipient.

[17] This is defined as areas for which the President declared a major disaster under the Stafford Act in response to Hurricane Sandy.

[18] The Notice of Funds Availability defines resiliency projects as those projects designed and built to address current and future vulnerabilities to a public transportation facility or system due to future occurrence or recurrence of emergencies or major disasters that are likely to occur in the geographic area in which the public transportation is located; or projected changes in development patterns, demographics, or climate change and extreme weather patterns.

[19] In December 2012, the President signed an executive order creating the Hurricane Sandy Rebuilding Task Force to ensure that the federal government continues to provide appropriate resources to support affected State, local, and tribal communities to improve the region's resilience, health, and prosperity by building for the future. 77 Fed. Reg. 74341 (Dec. 14, 2012). The Task Force is chaired by the Secretary of Housing and Urban Development and is comprised of representatives from other federal agencies.

[20] Hurricane Sandy Rebuilding Task Force, Hurricane Sandy Rebuilding Strategy: Stronger Communities, A Resilient Region (Washington, D. C.: August 2013).

[21] Department of Transportation, Office of Inspector General, MH-2014-008, Federal Transit Administration: Initial Assessment of FTA's Oversight of the Emergency Relief Program and Hurricane Sandy Relief Funds (Washington, D. C.: Dec. 3, 2013).

[22] The amount of Hazard Mitigation Grant Program funding available to an applicant is based upon the estimated total of Federal assistance, subject to the sliding scale formula outlined in section 5170c(a) of title 42, that FEMA provides for disaster recovery under the Presidential major disaster declaration. The formula provides for up to 15 percent of the first $2 billion of estimated aggregate amounts of disaster assistance, up to 10 percent for amounts between $2 billion and $10 billion, and up to 7.5 percent for amounts between $10 billion and $35.333 billion. For States with enhanced plans—FEMA approved state plans identifying policies and actions that can be implemented over the long term to reduce risks and future losses—the eligible assistance is up to 20 percent for estimated aggregate amounts of disaster assistance not to exceed $35.333 billion.

[23] FEMA may provide discretionary hazard mitigation funding under Section 406 of the Stafford Act which refers to FEMA's Public Assistance Program. Section 406 is applied to the parts of the facility that were actually damaged by the disaster and the mitigation measure provides protection from subsequent events. The mitigation work must be cost effective and be reasonably performed as part of the work or measure that will reduce the potential for damage to a facility from a disaster event. In addition, Community Development Block Grant Program (CDBG) funds—including Community Development Block Grant Disaster Recovery (CDBG–DR) funds may be used for the payment of the non-federal share required in connection with a federal grant-in-aid program (e.g., the FEMA Public Assistance Program) that provides funding for a CDBG-eligible activity.

[24] 49 C.F.R.§ 602.13(C)(5).

[25] 23 U.S.C. § 120(i)(1)(A).

[26] For some disasters, non-cash contributions referred to as "in-kind donations" may be credited toward the non-federal share of grant costs under FEMA's Public Assistance and Hazard Mitigation programs. In order for an in-kind contribution to be eligible for the nonfederal share, several conditions must apply such as that the contribution be necessary to accomplish the project objectives. Examples of in-kind contributions include property, services, equipment, and donated materials.

[27] GAO, Emergency Transit Assistance: Federal Funding for Recent Disasters, and Options for the Future, GAO-08-243, (Washington D.C.: Feb. 15, 2008) and GAO, Disaster Recovery: FEMA's Public Assistance Grant Program Experienced Challengers with Gulf Coast Rebuilding, GAO-09-129 (Washington, D. C.: Dec. 18, 2008).

[28] The total cost of a project funded through FHWA's Emergency Relief Program may not exceed the cost of repairing or constructing a facility that meets the current geometric and construction standards required for the types and volume of traffic that the facility will carry over its design life. Pub. L. No. 112-141, § 1107, codified at 23 U.S.C. § 125(d)(2).

[29] Pub. L. No. 113-2, div. B, 127 Stat. 4, 39-50.

[30] GAO, Highway Emergency Relief: Reexamination Needed to Address Fiscal Imbalance and Long-term Sustainability, GAO-07-245 (Washington D.C.: Feb. 23, 2007).

[31] GAO-08-243.

[32] GAO, Climate Change: Future Federal Adaptation Efforts Could Better Support Local Infrastructure Decision Makers, GAO-13-242 (Washington, D.C.: Apr. 12, 2013).

[33] GAO-13-242.

[34] FEMA has several Hazard Mitigation Assistance Grant Programs that provide funding for pre- and post-disaster mitigation. Some of FEMA's other hazard mitigation programs are not funded by the DRF. These programs include the Pre-disaster Mitigation Program and Flood Mitigation Assistance.

[35] For example, the President's Budget Request for the DRF for fiscal year 2009 was based on the 5-year average obligational level for non-catastrophic disaster activity (less estimates of funds carried forward and the amount of funds deobligated in prior years that can be used for new obligations for authorized purposes).

[36] Contract authority is the statutory authority to incur obligations in advance of an appropriation. Contract authority is unfunded, and a subsequent appropriation is needed to liquidate the obligation. FHWA obligates funds for a state project once FHWA approves a project. Subsequently, FHWA reimburses states out of the Highway Account of the Highway Trust Fund ("Highway Account") or the General Fund, depending on the source of funding. Congress can and has provided FHWA with supplemental appropriations, such as the DRAA, which are not funded through the Highway Trust Fund. The FHWA Emergency Relief Program is a reimbursable program—meaning FHWA reimburses the state for the federal share of the cost of the completed work assuming all federal requirements are met.

[37] 23 U.S.C. § 125.

[38] GAO-08-243.

[39] We also presented other options for Congress to consider such as 1) making permanent the temporary authorities that FTA was given to respond to the 2005 Gulf Coast hurricanes and (2) incorporating transit assistance as an eligible activity within FHWA's Emergency Relief Program. We also found that at the local and state level, mutual aid agreements between states and others can direct needed resources to transit agencies following a disaster.

[40] FEMA's Public Assistance Program does have an expedited payment process for debris removal and emergency protective measures. Under this process, FEMA will make payments for these activities within 60 days of completion of the estimated preliminary damage assessment and no later than 90 days after the pre-application was submitted. However, this funding is only available on a project-by-project basis, and FEMA is only able to release less than $1 million. Funding beyond $1 million would require OMB and congressional approval.

[41] GAO, High Risk Series: An Update, GAO-13-283 (Washington. D.C.: February 2013).

[42] GAO, Federal Disaster Assistance: Improved Criteria Needed to Assess a Jurisdiction's Capability to Respond and Recover on its Own, GAO-12-838 (Washington, D.C.: Sept. 12, 2012).

[43] GAO-07-245. In order to help put the FHWA Emergency Relief Program on a sustainable and more sound financial footing, we recommended among other things, that FHWA should, within its authority, tighten eligibility standards, recapture unused funds, and seek rescission of unneeded funds.

[44] GAO, Supplemental Appropriations: Opportunities Exist to Increase Transparency and Provide Additional Controls, GAO-08-314, (Washington D.C.: Jan. 31, 2008).

[45] Erskine Bowles, Alan Simpson et al., The Moment of Truth, Report of the National Commission on Fiscal Responsibility and Reform (December 2010).

[46] CRS, Disaster Relief Funding and Supplemental Appropriations for Disaster Relief, CRS Report, R40708 (Washington D.C.: Aug. 5, 2013).

[47] GAO, Results-Oriented Government: Practices That Can Help Enhance and Sustain Collaboration among Federal Agencies, GAO-06-15 (Washington, D.C.: October 2005).

[48] 49 U.S.C.§ 5324(c)(2).

[49] The President made major disaster declarations in the states of New Hampshire on March 19, 2013; Connecticut on March 21, 2013; Rhode Island on March 22, 2013; Maine on March 25, 2013; Massachusetts on April 19, 2013; and New York on April 23, 2013.

[50] GAO-06-15.

[51] GAO, Managing for Results: Implementation Approaches Used to Enhance Collaboration in Interagency Groups , GAO-14-220 (Washington, D.C.: Feb. 14, 2014).

[52] GAO-06-15.

# End Notes for Appendix I

[1] New Jersey Transit Corporation, Port Authority of New York and New Jersey, New York City Department of Transportation, New York Metropolitan Transportation Authority, Massachusetts Bay Transportation Authority, Southeastern Pennsylvania Transportation Authority, and Milford Connecticut Transit District.

[2] The National Railroad Passenger Corporation (Amtrak).

[3] During the review the team held coordination meetings with the DOT OIG. We learned they are conducting an extensive multi-phase review of how the FTA's Public Transportation Emergency Relief Program is being set up and FTA's efforts to ensure that DRAA funds are distributed appropriately. Thus, the team made a decision to focus our review on how the program is structured compared to previously established emergency relief programs in FEMA and FHWA instead of conducting an in-depth evaluation of FTA's Public Transportation Emergency Relief Program at this time.

[4] 42 U.S.C. §§ 5170, 5 170c, 5172; 44 C.F.R. Part 206.

[5] 49 U.S.C. § 5324; 49 C.F.R. Part 602.

[6] 23 U.S.C. §125 ; 23 C.F.R. Part 668.

[7] Congressional Research Service, Disaster Relief Funding and Supplemental Appropriations for Disaster Relief, August 5, 2013 and Erskine Bowles, Alan Simpson et al., The Moment of Truth, Report of the National Commission on Fiscal Responsibility and Reform (December 2010).

[8] GAO-07-245 and GAO-08-243.

[9] GAO-06-15.

[10] Department of Transportation, Office of Inspector General Audit Report, Initial Assessment of FTA's Oversight of the Emergency Relief Program and Hurricane Sandy Relief Funds, Federal Transit Administration, Report Number: MH-2104-008, (Washington, DC, Dec. 3, 2013).

# INDEX

## T

## U

## V

## W